EDUCATION FOR NONVIOLENCE

ALSO BY TORIN M. FINSER

Guided Self-Study
Rudolf Steiner's Path of Spiritual Development:
A Spiritual-Scientific Workbook

In Search of Ethical Leadership
If not now, when?

Initiative
A Rosicrucian Path of Leadership

Leadership Development
Change from the Inside Out

Organizational Integrity
How to Apply the Wisdom of the Body
to Develop Healthy Organizations

School as a Journey
The Eight-Year Odyssey of a Waldorf Teacher and His Class

School Renewal
A Spiritual Journey for Change

A Second Classroom
Parent–Teacher Relationships in a Waldorf School

Silence Is Complicity
A Call to Let Teachers Improve Our Schools
through Action Research—Not NCLB

Education *for* Nonviolence

The Waldorf Way

Torin M. Finser, PhD

SteinerBooks | 2017

STEINERBOOKS, 610 Main Street, Great Barrington, MA 01230
SteinerBooks, an imprint of Anthroposophic Press, Inc.
www.steinerbooks.org
© 2017 by Torin M. Finser.
All rights reserved

No part of this book may be reproduced, stored in a retrieval system, or transmitted in any form or by any means, electronic, mechanical, photocopying, recording, or otherwise, without the written permission of SteinerBooks. Design: Jens Jensen

Published with generous support from the
Waldorf Curriculum Fund

ISBN: 978-1-62148-198-0 (paperback)
ISBN: 978-1-62148-199-7 (eBook)

LIBRARY OF CONGRESS CONTROL NUMBER: 2017947802

Table of Contents

Introduction — vii

1. Loss of Childhood — 1
2. Ethical Judgment — 7
3. Evil — 10
4. Transformation through Sacrifice — 21
5. Character Education through Waldorf Education — 24
6. Sustainability — 34
7. Boys — 43
8. Education through the Senses — 63
9. Inclusive Recreation: Play — 76
10. Will — 88
11. Peace through Wholeness — 93
12. Unconditional Hospitality — 101
13. Forgiveness and the Last Supper — 110
14. Advocates of Nonviolence — 134
15. A Bill of Rights for Children — 144

Works Cited — 145

Acknowledgements — 147

This book is dedicated to our grandchildren:

Rowan Elizabeth Finser
Alexander Emmanuel Finser
Aviana Kista Regan Jensen

And to all the children who have the courage to enter the world at this time.

May our schools be worthy of them!

Introduction

The pictures we carry within us can be as important as the sights and sounds we take in through our senses. They help form our soul content; they either nourish or hinder our development. So it is ever so important what we carry as mental pictures. Throughout my life, the following have lived in my memory as sources of nourishment:

- Brussels: a city where my father worked for two years; the central square, La Grande-Place, surrounded by ornate buildings depicting the medieval guilds and houses of trade.
- Nice: a joyful city in the south of France, near my grandfather's summer home, vacations, music, and beaches.
- Orlando: the best way to enter the world of Disney and all the excitement that has brought joy to thousands of children over many, many years.
- Paris: the city of love, culture, wonderful restaurants (and many tourists!)

Then, suddenly, within the space of several months in 2015, one after another of these places became associated with horror, destruction, and wanton violence. Now when people refer to these cities, along with Dallas and others, they mean something quite different than the images I have carried all my life. What has happened to our world?

These days I rarely watch CNN anymore, and almost never listen to the news in the car. When I check up on things online, I often scroll down looking for something decent to read, something that will inspire, usually to no avail. What is happening to me? If I am unable to take it in anymore, what does that say about the state of our collective conscience?

My struggle with these horrible acts of violence has led me to look for the sources of such evil. The journey has taken me on philosophical pathways in a variety of directions. I went back to mythology and the content of the Waldorf curriculum. I contemplated the concept of betrayal in our modern lives and as it is represented in Leonardo's famous *Last Supper.*

But I could not simply continue going into the belly of the dragon; I needed a pathway of transformation. Building on *The Last Supper,* I spent time contemplating the mystery of transubstantiation, the change of substance. Is it possible to transform evil into good?

Images of my years as a Waldorf teacher began to flood back into my consciousness, and I realized, as never before, that Waldorf education is in fact a path of nonviolence. Through the rich story content, the arts, the continuity of relationships made possible with a guiding class teacher, the children are given both content and tools that can shape their character and the moral compass within each of them.

That led to the most profound riddle I have ever encountered: How can we as individuals practice forgiveness, unconditional hospitality, and boundless love precisely at this time, when the challenge is the greatest? Rather than becoming like the enemy by plotting revenge or another military solution, how can we cultivate a counter-force that is larger and more powerful and encompassing than those who seek to destroy humanity?

This book is meant to remind us of the importance of transformative education and to point out specific ways in which Waldorf works on character development. It ends with a call for political action and a very specific proposal for a Children's Bill of Rights that summarizes many of the key points of this book. We need collective action if we are to achieve a change in direction in the years ahead, and the best place to start is through the preservation of childhood.

1

Loss of Childhood

There are many ways in which our adult-focused civilization has conspired to rob children of their natural rights to childhood, and there have been wonderful testaments to this end over the years. For the purposes of this text, I would simply like to highlight a few of the symptoms.

1. Artificial chemicals affecting our children's bodies and behavior

Recent studies have shown that the use of artificial food colors can be an issue for "susceptible children with ADHD and other problem behaviors."* The FDA adds that, although they have not found a link between hyperactivity and the food dyes regarding the general population, "data suggest that [problem behaviors] may be exacerbated by exposure to a number of substances in food, including, but not limited to, artificial food colors" (ibid.). Parents need to be aware of dyes with names such as "yellow #5," found in cereals, macaroni and cheese, and numerous other food products. The makers of M&Ms say they have absolute confidence in the substances they use, while also indicating that they are continuing to explore the use of natural colors. Likewise, Kraft has begun to expand their product line to use organic white cheddar in macaroni and cheese.

Artificial colors are often cheap, stable, and bright, which helps marketing. While the authorities are reluctant to make

---

* *Wall Street Journal,* March 29, 2011, p. D1.

definitive statements due to difficulties with various studies, parents with a sound dose of common sense can fill in the gaps. If these substances cause the FDA to state that, "some kids are affected" (ibid., p. D2), then what about all the others that have not been measured? And what about the results of greater hyperactivity in classrooms, at home, and in social situations? It would seem that the food industry has focused on profits and marketing at the expense of children, which is evidenced by the increase of sugar in food products. Robbed of their natural way of playing outdoors, children are then given medications to compensate, thus enriching yet another industry.

2. Children are constantly being pulled out of class for individual work

In many schools today, there are a variety of specialists, and children are yanked in and out of classes regardless of what they are missing or what it does to the social context of the group. Children today are deprived of quiet time to play without interruption, to dream while gazing out a window, or to make up imaginative games. One little boy in a local kindergarten endured several math and reading classes while waiting for a chance to dress up and play a game that had been promised for later that morning. Finally, the time arrived, and he began to put on a costume and imagine the wonderful things he would do and say. Just as he started to play, the speech pathologist arrived and pulled him out of the class. He cried and cried—so much, in fact, that the entire speech session was wasted; nothing was accomplished. When he was finally returned to the class, the play session was over, and he was plunged into another reading group. Who can advocate for our children?

This over-individualization of education is yet another symptom of a loss of childhood. I remember spending hour after hour romping on the shore of a small lake during the summer, biking up and down the neighborhood, building igloos in the winter, and sitting high in a cherry tree in the late spring. Each scene in my inner eye is filled with other children. We were always doing things in groups. The long slope that was a meadow in the summer became a terrific toboggan hill in the winter as we piled on, sometimes three or four at a time, often falling off several times along the way. Even in school, we were one class, performing plays, reciting foreign language poems, or performing with our recorders at an assembly. Childhood was all about being together with other children. Parents and teachers often seemed to recede into the distance, always present but rarely front and center. There were days in the summer when I ran outside after breakfast and would return home only for the very basic necessity of food.

Children need other children. In those days of play and intense activity, we learned how to get along, resolve conflicts, problem solve, and negotiate. These play-to-learn years were essential in helping us develop life skills that have proven ever so helpful later on. No standardized test has ever measured these skills, and no textbook has ever taught me as much in this realm as did the time spent with other children.

Now we live in a world of IEPs, assessment, learning outcomes, and rubrics. So much individual attention has robbed children of the experience of being part of a whole. The curriculum is divided and subdivided into separate subjects and learning goals. Along the way, we lose sight of the whole, the integrated web of life that is interdependent. Are our children happier? Are they healthier? Are they learning more?

I fear the answer to these key questions is one unqualified "No." So why are we subjecting our children to this torture? The pain on their faces and the stomachaches all speak to the silent protest of so many young ones who cannot decipher the reasoning behind the complex machinations imposed upon them by an adult-centered world. The individualization of childhood is a crime against humanity. Politicians who know little of sound educational practices pass laws that force teachers to do things common sense would otherwise reject. Arts, games, foreign languages, outdoor education are all shunted aside, and the young learners are left with more drills, flip charts, pre-digested questions, and an abstract construct of the world. We have lost any perspective of the whole—the whole child, the whole environment, the whole multidimensional and multifaceted world of nature and age appropriate learning. We are losing our children and, with them, the possibility of social renewal.

3. *Childhood is supposed to be a basis for future relationships*

My childhood friends were not always easy on me; at times, I took sanctuary in the safety of books and the inner world of imaginary relationships. Yet I was fortunate to attend schools (Waldorf for ten years) that for the most part valued community and gave us opportunities to develop lasting relationships since my class stayed together with one class teacher for eight years. Now when I look back on forty-plus years in the workplace, I see that it was the relationship skills I developed as a student that have helped me more than anything that can be measured on a standardized test. Teamwork, problem solving, communication, conflict resolution, and negotiating are all skills that have very little value in the mindset of No Child Left Behind (NCLB), Common Core, or SATs. We are not only missing the train with our educational practices, but also the entire train station.... We are not even remotely near any relevant geographical location! No wonder so many prominent business leaders feel that the workers they have to choose from are unqualified.

Recently, while surfing the web, I came across some statements by Margaret Wheatley made in 2006 in, "Relationship: The Basic Building Blocks of Life."[*] Except for Rudolf Steiner, she is perhaps my most frequently quoted source, as her view of organizations is helpful. Thus, I was thrilled to read these two following paragraphs, which go to the heart of the theme of relationships:

> The scientific search for the basic building blocks of life has revealed a startling fact: there are none. The deeper that physicists peer into the nature of reality, the only thing they find is relationships. Even subatomic particles do not exist alone. One physicist described neutrons, electrons, etc. as "...a set of relationships that reach outward to other things." Although physicists still name them as separate, these particles aren't ever visible until they're in relationship with other particles. Everything in the Universe is composed of these "bundles of potentiality" that only manifest their potential in relationship.
>
> We live in a culture that does not acknowledge this scientific fact. We believe wholeheartedly in the individual and build organizations based on this erroneous idea. We create organizational charts of separate boxes, with lines connecting the boxes that indicate reporting relationships and alleged channels of communication. But our neatly drawn organizations are as fictitious as building blocks to physicists. The only form of organization used on this planet is the network—webs of interconnected, interdependent relationships. This is true for human organizations as well. Whatever boxes we stuff staff into, people always reach out to those who will give them information, be their allies, offer support or cheer them up. Those lines and boxes are imaginary. The real organization is always a dense network of relationships." (Wheatley, 2006)

---

[*] At http://www.margaretwheatley.com/articles/relationships.html (accessed July 4, 2017).

4. We have forgotten to let our children breathe!

Although popular literature is filled with advice on how adults can slow down, there are still all too few instances of applying that very same wisdom to child rearing or schooling. Sometimes starting at a very early age, children are shuttled between after school music lessons, tutoring, dance lessons, and sports, only to come home for a rushed dinner and homework.

At school, forty-five-minute lessons continue the conspiracy against slowing down. Each class contains a welter of material and activities only to have the bell ring and it begins again with a different teacher. The emphasis is on wakefulness, attention, and retention. Many teachers know that this is not healthy, but they feel powerless to make changes to the system. In the rush to test and meet core curriculum standards, we have left out much of a chance for children to be children.

Waldorf education is an effort to address these issues from the earliest years on. The chapters that follow contain several pathways for restoring our commitment to the preservation of childhood.

2

Ethical Judgment

There is an inner component to the loss of childhood that is often overlooked in public discourse—loss of the arts in our curriculum, absence of play and the outdoors, storytelling, and so on—which has led to deficits in character education. Many young children are growing up with less and less ability to tell right from wrong.

We see symptoms of this in daily news accounts of school violence, bullying, and other forms of antisocial behavior. Children seem to have less and less ability to self-reflect and judge their own actions. Their thoughts are often not tempered by adequate emotional intelligence. Abstract ideas, often fixed, seem to go straight into impulsive actions. This can so easily happen when feelings are not engaged and empathy not fostered in the early years.

Many who first encounter Waldorf education see an opportunity to protect childhood. As parents get to know the curriculum better, they begin to discover that a Waldorf school is not just a safe environment but also schooling in ethical judgment. Stories and history lessons are rich in character development. Individuals go through trials and crises that provide invaluable opportunities for personal growth. Through phenomenology, the sciences foster objectivity, and math trains clear thinking. The arts develop aesthetic sensitivity and sound judgment. Foreign languages and immersion in various cultures from around the world foster social sensitivity. English and literature lessons build problem solving skills and the art of verbal and written expression. These are all capacities that enhance human development and are ever so important in the workplace. They all have one thing in common: validation of the universally human and the dignity of each and every person on this Earth.

Waldorf educators are not alone in recognizing the importance of ethical judgment, or what others have called moral reasoning. Kohlberg supplied the idea of stages of moral reasoning. At the lowest or "pre-conventional" level, moral judgment rests primarily on perceived consequences: an action is right if you are rewarded and wrong if you are punished. In the intermediate or "conventional" level, the emphasis is on conforming to authority and following the rules. At the highest or "post-conventional" level, ethical judgment rests upon general principles: the greatest good for the greatest number, or universal moral principles (Bolman and Deal p. 220).

These questions embody four important principles of moral judgment:

- *Mutuality: Are all parties to a relationship operating under the same understanding about the rules of the game?*

  Enron's Ken Ley was talking up the company's stock to analysts and employees even as he and others were selling their shares. In the period when WorldCom improved its profits by cooking the books, it made its competitors look bad. Top executives at competing firms such as AT&T and Sprint felt the heat from analysts and shareholders and wondered, "Why can't we get the results they're getting?" Only later did they learn the answer: "They're cheating, and we're not."

- *Generality: Does a specific action follow a principle of moral conduct applicable to all comparable situations?*

When Enron and WorldCom violated accounting principles to inflate their results, they were secretly breaking the rules, not adhering to a broadly applicable rule of conduct.

- *Openness: Are we willing to make our thinking and decisions public and confrontable?*

    As Justice Louis Brandeis observed in his book *Other People's Money and How the Bankers Use It,* "Sunlight is said to be the best of disinfectants."

- *Caring: Does this action show concern for the legitimate interests and feelings of others?*

    Enron's effort to protect its share price by locking in employees so they couldn't sell their Enron shares in their retirement accounts, even as the value of the shares plunged, put the interests of senior executives ahead of everyone else's. (Bolman and Deal, pp 221–222)

Mutuality, generality, openness, and caring. These are precisely the qualities our world today needs more than ever! Many of these themes will be developed in subsequent chapters later in this book.

3

Evil

Some time ago, students at the Monadnock Waldorf High School in Keene, New Hampshire, offered several performances of Shakespeare's *Macbeth*. I had the good fortune of attending two of them! In this remarkable drama of betrayal, murder, sinister witches, human despair, and layer upon layer of evil, Shakespeare speaks to themes that resonate today more than ever. Now, we have different actors on the world stage, but the encounter with evil persists with devastating regularity, and the anguished question in Shakespeare's drama remains seemingly unanswered:

> Canst thou not minister to a mind diseased,
> Pluck from the memory a rooted sorrow,
> Raze out the written troubles of the brain,
> And with some sweet oblivious antidote
> Cleanse the stuffed bosom of that perilous stuff
> Which weighs upon the heart? (Macbeth, p.22)

Despite heroic efforts over centuries, "that perilous stuff" still weighs upon the heart of mankind. Why is evil so intricately bound up with the human condition? Are we at a crisis point? How can Anthroposophy help us go beyond the platitudes and hand wringing on the evening news?

In *Macbeth*, Shakespeare continues along a path of distinctive seven-year periods that led him to early success with his comedies and then a cathartic moment at age 35 when he lost a good friend and patron. What followed were the tragedies *Hamlet*,

Othello, *King Lear*, and *Macbeth*. These dramas were composed at a time in his life we call the "consciousness soul." One aspect of this period involves the human encounter with the Self in all its dimensions. Perhaps no other art form is better suited to portray the forces of catharsis in the human soul as is possible in drama and the spoken word.

The human connection to the spiritual world in *Macbeth* is tenuous at best, and then only in the form of prophecy and the sinister words of the three witches. They can be seen as three counter-forms of unredeemed aspects of the human soul, and their leader, Hecate, the counter-form of the human "I" (Hiebel, p. 37). The prophecies that Macbeth takes so literally (Birnam Wood and "not of women born") turns out other than he expected. The abstract idea becomes, through lived experience, a painful awakener of consciousness: "To know my deed, 'twere best not to know myself." Through death, first Lady Macbeth and then Macbeth himself find release from inner torment. A death process is part of the awakening of the consciousness soul, if not for Macbeth, then at least for a comprehending audience.

In a lecture given on October 26, 1918, Rudolf Steiner speaks of two great mysteries connected with the development of the consciousness soul: "The Mystery of Death and the Mystery of Evil."* The death forces otherwise active in the universe are now available to mankind, in part to help us, "think precisely in matters of importance" (p. 115). There is so much error in common thinking today that it is hard to penetrate to the real causes of events we hear of (i.e., in the news). The way forward is developing new clarity of thinking which will make it possible to receive the forces of Spirit Self, Life Spirit, and Spirit

---

* Steiner, *From Symptom to Reality in Modern History*, p. 114

Body (or Spirit Man). To do this in the fifth post-Atlantean epoch, human beings must "fully unite their being with the forces of death" (p. 117).

Likewise, with evil we cannot just fixate on evil all around us but need to look at evil tendencies within each of us. "Basically, all human evil proceeds from what we call egoism" (Steiner, *Evil*, p. 25). In fact, Rudolf Steiner is quite emphatic that these tendencies are, "present in all human beings" (p. 118). Evil action is, of course, another matter and much has occurred on the world stage due to what has been, "perverted by the social order" (p. 118). Once again, these forces of evil are there to help humankind, "break through to the life of the spirit at the level of the consciousness soul" (p. 118).

I have taken up some of these indications as I watch CNN or read of the latest atrocities portrayed in newspapers or on the Internet. After the customary reactions of disbelief, anguish, and shock, I have tried to look for evidence of this awakening to the life of the Spirit. It is not easy at first, but when taking a walk later in the day, and particularly when one carries an issue over a few nights of sleep, something can start to happen in the life of the Soul. One starts to ask: What is happening to humanity? Why are we bombarded with so many experiences of death and evil? Why have so many people stopped being human? This then led me to wonder about conscience.

There may be many who can speak to this topic more eloquently, but for me conscience has to do with the inner compass, that point within where one can weigh and evaluate actions, thoughts, and feelings. Even a young child will often show a remarkable ability to speak out of this place of conscience such as, "Mommy, I am so sorry I broke your favorite coffee mug." If a three-year-old can listen to this inner voice, why can't we?

It is easy, perhaps, to just turn off the news and leave the newspaper on the doorstep. But it is for some reason that I am on this Earth at this particular time and I feel an inner obligation to stay connected, even affirm that I too am part of this world, and as such, I have some responsibility for the state of humanity. If I am connected, then what happens in Missouri and in Paris is part of me. I am inwardly revolted at the all too many instances of racism that are still evident today (and not only on some college campuses). I am speechless at the frequent and wanton acts of terrorism around the world and mystified by the fundamentalist tilt in world religions. My heart aches when friends and neighbors suffer loss due to drugs and addiction. And out of this, struggle something emerges that we can call the voice of conscience.

One of the reasons I entered the teaching profession many years ago, and have continued as a faculty member in the Education Department at Antioch University New England, is that education in all its dimensions is needed more than ever. Learning is all about seeing other perspectives, looking for layers of meaning, and developing understanding. It is good to be passionate about something, but that passion needs to be tempered (or enhanced) with knowledge. This is what is so often lacking in antisocial behavior today.

Is it not puzzling that over time acts of violence and horrendous wars have been perpetrated in the name of one religion or another? Fundamentalism has been with humankind for a long time, but somewhere along the way, we seem to have forgotten that the voice of God can also be heard in the stirring of human conscience.

It seems humanity is being challenged to wake up and see that we are all in this together. Every time we judge someone else (something also known to students of Anthroposophy), we are embarking on a path that can lead downhill. Instead, we need to reach out to the many others on this Earth who are also convinced that there must be a better way. We need to come together and be willing to hear the voices of those who are different and have different views than our own. Tolerance is but a first step; necessary, but not sufficient. Being human means stretching ourselves to see the universal, or eternal, in others. We need to engage at a different level including nonviolent solutions to shared challenges. We need to talk less and listen more, including the deep listening that opens doors for the tender voice of conscience.

And so at the end of the previously cited lecture in *Symptom to Reality*, Rudolf Steiner gives us a few very practical yet deeply significant steps forward toward creating a new, more humane culture on this Earth:

1. We can work to develop the capacity to comprehend a human being symbolically. We need to learn to perceive the archetype of a person through his or her picture-nature, a warm appreciation of the other.
2. We need to develop a new sense for language and the capacity to feel, to sense our neighbor through the spoken word. It will not be the exact words that matter, but rather the sensing of the region of soul from whence they come, the colors of words. Thus a new capacity for listening will emerge.
3. Then one can work on sensing the emotional reactions of others to such a degree that respiration will change, one will breathe differently when in contact with one person than with another.
4. Finally, and most difficult to understand, is the indication that in the realm of the will one will be able to "digest" the

deeds of others, to process them in a way that awakens new comprehension of the other human being. (pp. 124–126)

One could summarize by saying that in the development of the consciousness soul, human beings will learn to experience one another through warmth, the color of language, through respiration, and through digestion of will impulses. This is precisely what was prophetically present in so many of Shakespeare's plays, and what has unfolded again and again in the 400 years since his death on April 23, 1616. It is the modern dilemma: How can we continue to evolve toward greater and greater consciousness of our universal humanity? Death and even the presence of evil on this Earth are in fact wise teachers that awaken the human conscience, and help us on the path toward being human.

Even though we err throughout life, our striving in the end can lift us up again:

> MEPHISTOPHELES:
> "You'll lose him yet! I offer bet and tally,
> Provided that your Honor gives
> Me leave to lead him gently up my alley!
>
> THE LORD:
> "So long as on the Earth he lives,
> So long it shall not be forbidden.
> Man ever errs the while he strives."
> *Faust, Prologue in Heaven.*

So, what can we do to overcome evil?

This question has lived with humanity for centuries, indeed ever since the Fall from Paradise. Now more than ever, we long to see some transformation, redemption, some sign of hope. And once one begins to look for it, both within and without, it is possible to find examples of this transformation. They are, in fact, all around us: in nature, art, and literature. The key ingredient is the human being. As Goethe once said, "If you treat a person as he is, he will remain the same. But treat a person as he ought to be, he will become better" (paraphrased). There is perhaps no better example of this than in chapter twelve of Victor Hugo's *Les Misérables:*

THE BISHOP AT WORK

The next day at sunrise, Monseigneur Bienvenu was walking in the garden. Madame Magloire ran toward him quite beside himself.

"Monseigneur, Monseigneur," she cried, "Does Your Lordship know where the silver basket is?"

"Yes," said the bishop.

"God be praised!" she said. "I did not know what had become of it."

The Bishop had just found the basket on a flowerbed. He gave it to Madame Magloire and said, "Here it is."

"Yes," she said, "but there's nothing in it. Where's the silver?"

"Ah!" said the bishop. "It's the silver then that troubles you. I don't know where that is."

"Good heavens! It's stolen. That man who came last night stole it!"

And in the twinkling of an eye, with all the agility of her age, Madame Magloire ran to the oratory, went into the alcove, and came back to the bishop. The bishop was bending with some sadness over a cochlearia des Guillons, which the basket had broken in falling. At Madame Maggiore's cry he looked up.

"Monseigneur, the man has gone! The silver is stolen!"

While she was uttering this exclamation, her eyes fell on a corner of the garden where she saw traces of the escape. A capstone of the wall had been dislodged. "See, that is where he got out; he jumped in the Cochefilet Lane. The wretch! He stole our silver!"

The bishop was silent for a moment; then raising his serious eyes, he said to Madame Magloire, "Now first, did this silver belong to us?"

Madame Magloire was speechless. After a moment the bishop continued, "Madame Magloire, for a long time I have wrongfully been withholding this silver. It belonged to the poor. Who was this man? A poor man, quite clearly."

"Alas! Alas!" returned Madame Magloire. "It's not on my account or Mademoiselle's; it is all the same to us. But it's for you Monseigneur. What is monsieur going to eat with now?" (p. 102, Hugo)

The bishop looked at her with amazement. "But don't we have any pewter cutlery?" Madame Magloire shrugged her shoulders. "Pewter smells."

"Well, then, iron."

Madame Magloire grimaced. "Iron has a taste."

"Well, then," said the bishop, "wooden implements."

In a few minutes he was breakfasting at the table where Jean Valjean sat the night before. While breakfasting, Monseigneur Bienvenu pleasantly remarked to his sister, who said nothing, and Madame Magloire, who was grumbling to herself, that there was really no need even of a wooden spoon or fork to dip a piece of bread into a cup of milk.

"Was there ever such an idea?" said Madame Magloire to herself, as she went back and forth: "to take in a man like that, and to give him a bed at his side; and yet what a blessing he did nothing but steal! Oh, good Lord! It gives me the chills just to think of it!"

As the brother and sister were rising from the table, there was a knock at the door.

"Come in," said the bishop.

The door opened. A strange, fierce group appeared on the threshold. Three men were holding a fourth by the collar. The three men were gendarmes; the fourth, Jean Valjean.

A brigadier of gendarmes, who appeared to head the group, was near the door. He advanced toward the bishop, giving a military salute.

"Monseigneur," he said.

At this word, Jean Valjean, who was sullen and seemed entirely dejected, raised his head with a stupefied air. "Monseigneur!" he murmured. "Then it is not the curé!"

"Silence!" said a gendarme. "It is his lordship, the bishop."

In the meantime Monseigneur Bienvenu had approached as quickly as his great age permitted: "Ah, there you are!" he said looking at Jean Valjean. "I'm glad to see you. But I gave you the candlesticks, too, which are silver like the rest and would bring two hundred francs. Why didn't you take them along with your cutlery?"

Jean Valjean opened his eyes and looked at the bishop with an expression no human could describe.

"Monseigneur," said the brigadier, "then what this man said was true? We met him. He was acting like a fugitive and we arrested him to find out. He had this silver."

"And he told you," interrupted the bishop, with a smile, "that it had been given to him by a good old priest at whose house he had slept. I see it all. And you brought him back here? It's all a mistake."

"If that is so," said the brigadier, "we can let him go."

"Please do," replied and the bishop. The gendarmes released Jean Valjean, who shrank back.

"Is it true they're letting me go?" He murmured, as if talking in his sleep.

"Yes! You can go. Don't you understand?" said the gendarme.

"My friend," said the bishop, "before you go away, here are your candlesticks; take them."

He went to the mantelpiece, took the two candlesticks, and handed them to Jean Valjean. The two women observed without a word, gesture, or look that could disturb the bishop.

Jean Valjean was trembling all over. He took the two candlesticks distractedly, with a bewildered expression.

"Now," said the bishop," go into peace. By the way my friend, when you come again, you needn't come through the garden. You can always come and go by the front door. It is only closed with the latch, day or night."

Then turning to the gendarmes, he said, "Messieurs, you may go." The gendarmes left. John Valjean felt like a man about to faint.

The bishop approached him and said, in a low voice, "Do not forget, ever, that you have promised me to use the silver to become an honest man."

Jean Valjean, who had no recollection of any such promise, stood dumbfounded. The bishop had stressed these words as he spoke them. He continued, solemnly, "Jean Valjean, my brother, you no longer belong to evil, but to good. It is your soul I am buying for you. I withdraw it from the dark thoughts and from the Spirit of perdition, and I give it to God!" (Hugo pp. 103–104),

❋

You no longer belong to evil, but to good. What an amazing example! The silver, even the candlesticks, are donated to save the common thief, Jean Valjean, who had already spent years in hard labor and had his share of resentments and anger. With one deed, the bishop turns a life around, and Jean Valjean goes on to be an outstanding citizen and father for the rest of his life.

What so often corrupts, money and silver, is actually put to use for the good. This story reminds me of the three temptations in the wilderness as told by Matthew (4:1–11) and Luke (4:1–13). The temptation I have puzzled over the most is when the devil asks Christ to turn stones into bread. According to Rudolf Steiner in his lectures published as *The Fifth Gospel*, this temptation was not fully resolved with the words "Men do not live by bread alone." The worldly practice of earning gold or money was foreign to Christ: "He did not know that there below it was necessary to turn mineral substance—metal—into money, into bread. Ahriman had said that men on the Earth below had to nourish themselves by means of gold. That was the point where Ahriman still retained power. And he said: I shall use this power!" (Steiner, *The Fifth Gospel*, p 96). In his path of loneliness, the Christ was not yet fully part of the Earth and had not experienced "by the sweat of thy brow" work on the Earth. To this day, Ahriman and evil have a particular doorway into the human soul through money. This then led me to look at ways in which humanity has tried to overcome the grip of money, food, belongings, and that led me to the literature on unconditional hospitality.

4

Transformation through Sacrifice

"Human beings ever err the while they strive." A curious phrase indeed. Human beings continually err, but in striving, even blindly at times, there is an eternal possibility of transformation. If evil is a fact of our modern world, the issue is not a matter of avoidance or even victory, but rather of transformation. Avoiding evil can only be temporary, and is really just an option for the select few who might indulge in the illusion of protection behind gated communities and electronic surveillance. And victory achieved through military means usually begets more hardship, resentment, and, ultimately, forces that work toward revenge leading to a never-ending cycle of violence.

If it is not possible to completely avoid violence in today's word, or to totally overcome evil, what can be done? As with most things in life, it helps to go to the source. In this case, the source of evil is in the human soul, the psyche, the inner life of a person. The life of emotions, of anger, fear, and envy are real forces that work their way outward from within. If one is to get at the root of evil, one has to begin with the soul.

M. Scott Peck describes in *Children of the Lie* numerous examples and case studies a variety of patients he treated over the years who suffered from one sort of affliction or another. In several cases there are vivid portrayals of children and adults whose inner turmoil led to various forms of evil. In one instance, for example, he describes a boy who lost his brother to suicide. It was not only that terrible loss that led to counseling, but the misunderstanding of his parents and their attitudes that seriously compromised the boy's emotional life. The inner battles were not recognized until Peck was able to provide treatment, which in this case included sending the boy to live with a relative for a while. The parents had to let go.

In this chapter, I focus on one key antidote that works more strongly than any prescription drug or medical intervention does for physical illness. It is an antidote that works from within outward—from the soul into the social life of community. It is expressed with one simple but ever-so potent word: *sacrifice*.

Sacrifice in Everyday Life

When one stops to think of it, most people today make countless daily sacrifices:

- The teacher who stays after school to help a student with those perplexing math problems.
- A parent who gets up in the middle of the night to hold their child with the flu, put on new pajamas, change the sheets if needed, and then tries to get a few hours of sleep before dawn.
- The nurse who circles back one more time, even after their shift has ended, to check on a patient.
- The kid at school who shares his lunch, even if it is favorite meal.

The examples are numerous if one but stops to observe. The small deeds are an integral part of the social fabric of a home, school or community. What happens when someone performs a selfless deed? Even if very small, the person who is giving steps out of the normal, small confines of "self" and enters a more active relationship with the "other." One gives over something of one's everyday self and takes a step beyond. The world, or the other person, mirrors back something of what has been given, and a new perspective is won. In short, we see ourselves differently during and after a selfless deed. We can look in on our self as someone from outside, seeing both the strengths and imperfections with new objectivity.

In the process of giving and receiving back, warmth is generated. The teacher leaving the school an hour late may be ever so tired, but also has a good feeling inside. The parent crawling back into bed at 3 a.m. may not be able to think straight, but feels ever so connected to the sick child. In all cases where there is no ulterior motive but purely a wish to serve, sacrifice generates warmth. Warmth of heart can give the soul new strength, passion, integrity, and courage. Warmth generated through sacrifice and service is an antidote to all that is wrong in this world. One has only to study the lives of great people to see this in practice. Those public servants, those who led social movements and brought about real change were often people who were willing to make great sacrifices against all odds.

Sacrifice gives human beings new inner resources that can move worlds. The force of good human intention can make a difference in countering evil. For those forces that want evil to rule also count on human passivity and apathy. Each act of violence we witness or see on the news is a call to the human spirit. This call is not one that asks us to bear arms and fight (although defense is often appropriate), but most of all the call is to wake up and do something for someone close at hand. A selfless deed in a local community is a beam of light shooting around the world. One deed of love can reverberate around the globe.

5

CHARACTER EDUCATION THROUGH WALDORF EDUCATION

It is commonly known that exercise helps prevent many illnesses, as does good nutrition and good sleep. What is not so often discussed is the role of education in relation to emotional health and violence prevention. Although I am not a criminologist or psychologist, I have spent years in education and have had time to observe cases of success or failure. Many children grow up to be healthy, well-adjusted adults, but a few do not. Why?

In the movie *Trading Places*, the debate of nature vs. nurture is played out in an entertaining drama. When a pair of scheming old men in a brokerage house decide to engineer the swap of a younger trader with a homeless man, the role of environment and wealth ends up playing a crucial role in the change of personality. But is the environment the only crucial element? Are some people born with fewer possibilities? These questions will no doubt rage into the future, but for the purposes of this chapter, I want to look at the role of education in shaping a person's life. All the discussion about test scores and college placement obscures the fundamental issue of character education and its crucial role in developing mature judgment and sound decision making.

To begin with, let us look at the some of the most commonly mentioned characteristics of a person who commits a violent act. (I choose to focus on the individual and not on issues such as war or genocide, which is beyond the scope of this contribution.) If one reads the accounts of those who commit random acts of violence, such as mass-shooting incidents, the following are often reported: varying degrees of isolation, a propensity toward fixed ideas, instances of emotional blockage, low self-esteem, feelings of helplessness with few options, loss of family ties, depression, a series of bad choices that cascade into serious issues, and a tendency to live in a fictional world of semblance and illusion. No doubt there are more, but for the purposes of this chapter, I will look at some of these and indicate ways in which they changed over the past few decades, from issues around television to video games to social media; but the effects of too much sedentary time in front of any screen remain the same. Young children need to get out into nature, explore, do things, play with peers, and be engaged in real time activities. But most of all, from the point of view of this book, the content of most video games can be highly damaging. Violence, attitudes toward women and minorities, sound effects, and addiction to gaming can seriously impact schoolwork and health. If we want a society that is less violent, we need to seriously limit exposure to the media and support our Waldorf schools in providing a rich array of alternative activities. (See later chapter on boys)

Community

In a Waldorf school, a group of children stay together for many years. Although there may be some coming and going, especially after kindergarten and the grade school, for the most part students in a Waldorf school get to experience continuity of relationship (See School as a Journey). They learn a variety of subjects together, eat lunches in their homeroom, play together at recess, do class plays, struggle together when there is a classroom challenge, and celebrate the rites of passage together. All this builds stability, a sense of safety, and shared responsibility. After a while, my students rarely said, "I did well." More often they said, "We did well." This experience of community teaches countless lessons that can help with relationships and working together later in life.

Interdisciplinary Learning

Unlike many schools in which students learn isolated subjects in forty-five-minute periods, Waldorf teachers emphasize interdisciplinary learning. What this means is that the sixth grade class teacher who has done a three- to four-week main lesson block in business math will then teach English skills with emphasis on letter writing, job applications, and so on. Or, after teaching mineralogy and geology, they may do a unit on South American geography. The history of Rome is also full of opportunities for writing essays, and physics includes mathematics. But even beyond one year, which other schools also attempt to do, by "looping," or teaching many years to the same group, subjects can be related to one another over time. I remember doing numbers in first grade in a way that was mindful of the algebra lessons that would come many years later. Waldorf is interdisciplinary and integrated. Knowledge does not come in separate boxes, but is related again and again to the human being and to actual life situations. Thus, students learn problem solving and contextual thinking that is more attuned to real work situations than the traditional segregation of subjects. They learn to see the world holistically and realistically.

Crafts and Practical Skills

One of the earliest impressions visitors to a Waldorf school will have has to do with the practical activities and skills that are a part of every day. From bread baking in kindergarten to knitting a scarf in first grade, carving wooden spoons in fifth to sewing shirts in eighth, students enjoy a vigorous curriculum in the crafts. In main lessons (the first two hours of each day) students make their own textbooks, model Egyptian pyramids, paint in botany, and sketch their science experiments. They are always doing meaningful things with their hands. Through these focused activities children learn to harness their will-forces, channel their energy and create beautiful objects that give them tremendous satisfaction. My favorite birthday presents over the years have been gifts from our children that they made with their own hands. Along the way, they gained many skills that built confidence. Waldorf graduates are often known for the "can-do" mentality. If one has learned to make things, even when they are difficult or frustrating at times, one has the capacity later in life to solve problems and tackle new challenges with confidence (see chapter 10, on educating the will and morality).

Cooperative Games, Morning Circle, and More

Much of the world today sees things in terms of competition: nation states, politics, sports, college acceptances, etc. Many schools, and certainly public attitudes, are focused on test scores, which promote competition. Yet when people end up actually working in real jobs, test scores and grades have little to do with success. Instead, much depends on teamwork, collaboration, and networking. Thus Waldorf schools try and minimize competition, rarely test in the early grades, and focus instead on cooperation. Examples include the morning circle in the main lesson in which children sing, practice times tables, do country-dances, and celebrate seasonal activities. Outdoors, many Waldorf schools still do hop scotch, tag games, handball, and other "old fashioned" activities that promote teamwork and dexterity. Much of the formal learning in a classroom is done with the participation of the entire group rather than individual worksheets and lesson plans. All this is intentional: the hope is to graduate students who love to participate actively, network naturally, and problem solve together.

Reverence for Nature

Rather than a few minutes outdoors, Waldorf schools embrace the wonderful instructive opportunities found in the natural world. Forest-based kindergartens have been part of Waldorf early-childhood programs for years, third grades plant gardens, and every year there are increasingly challenging field trips (for more, see chapter 8, on sensory education).

Limiting Media

Waldorf schools have long been advocates of limiting exposure to the media in all forms, especially in the early childhood and elementary grades. The types of possible exposure have issues such as rudeness and churlishness and behaving differently from what they actually are can be particularly obvious in the behavior of boys. Coupled then with shame and uncertain feelings of self-worth, one then has a fertile seedbed for radical ideas and false idols. Boys in particular can become fixated on a simplistic solution and when the key ingredients of poverty, shame, low self-worth, and idolization of a political or religious idea all come together, one has a lethal cocktail that can show up on CNN as another car bomb or mass shooting.

Much of this has to do with suppressed feelings that rise into semi-consciousness. I say "semi," because if a person were really conscious of the effects of violence, it would be much harder to be the instrument of such cruelty. But in the case of those young men, and increasingly also women and children, who take up violent acts, there is evidence of a feeling life that is cramped and mental pictures and abstract ideas that are fixed and absolute. Steiner speaks of the astral body (feelings leading to conscious thoughts) that needs to be ruled by the "I," our true Self. Young people are developmentally striving for that inner ruler, but it takes time, even for those of us who are older. Along the way, there are many bumps in the road.

The Right Time- and Age-Appropriate Curriculum

Rudolf Steiner articulated a highly differentiated view of child development that can be found in his first lecture on education, *The Education of the Child*, and in many of his subsequent lecture courses, including *The Kingdom of Childhood, A Child's Changing Consciousness*, and many others. Based on this comprehensive picture of child development, the Waldorf curriculum unfolds in a way that is intended to meet the particular needs of a child at each stage. So for example, when children live strongly in an imaginative consciousness at six and seven, reading and arithmetic are introduced through a wide variety of fairy tales and fables. When later on the sixth grader stands firmly on the Earth with a strong sense of cause and effect, students are introduced to laws of physics. If one were to switch these subjects around and, say, teach physics to seven-year-olds and fairy tales to twelve-year-olds, it would simply not fly. Moreover, when the curriculum is age appropriate, the material goes so much further; the students really respond. When a subject meets with student interest, it is remembered and integrated into life. It is like the difference between seeing a movie of Australia and actually going there. Living an experience is much more valuable and memorable! And when students feel "met," they are much more likely to be secure and confident.

Individual Attention

All this happens under the guidance of teachers who work hard to meet the individual needs of their students. A Waldorf teacher spends countless hours preparing lessons intended both for the group and for the individual needs of their students. Thus, for example, using the four temperaments and knowledge of different learning styles, a Waldorf teacher might tell the story of Queen Elizabeth I with different children in mind. When describing her elaborate costumes, the teacher might focus particularly on the sanguine children, who love such detail. Or when narrating the dramatic events of the Spanish Armada, one might want to be near the choleric children, who love battles and ships on fire. The melancholic will mourn the death of Mary Stuart and Elizabeth's ambivalent relationship to that fateful decision. And the phlegmatic children will pay careful attention to Elizabeth's lavish parties and the wide assortment of delicious things to eat. One story told to one group of seventh graders might meet the individual learning needs of many different students. Then there are the many hours a Waldorf teacher spends working individually with students on their compositions, geography projects, play performances, and much more. Students in a Waldorf school often receive extraordinary special attention, and not just because classes tend to be smaller. And all this individual attention helps a student feel supported, recognized, and validated.

Emotional Intelligence

Many of the cited characteristics, along with the arts and the social curriculum of learning together over many years, all support the development of emotional intelligence. Feelings can be processed, developed, and transformed through painting, singing, drama, movement, and the creation of the ever-so-beautiful main lesson books. Waldorf children have issues and struggles, as do most children on the Earth these days, but there is a chance for the gradual unfolding of emotional health in a loving environment that focuses on the good, beautiful, and true, a school resplendent in the arts, and a class in which each child really matters as a human being and not as a percentile. We know that emotional intelligence is yet another crucial factor in preparing a more peace-loving future world.

Parent Involvement

Countless studies have shown that children benefit when parents are involved in their education. Most schools I have known—public, charter, Montessori, Waldorf—have a cadre of dedicated parents who volunteer and come to meetings. Unfortunately, all too often this group represents a small percentage of the total parent population of a given school. The same parents (mostly mothers) show up at events, and some are seen only when their child is in a special artistic performance or athletic event. By their very nature and founding, more parents tend to get involved in charter schools than regional public schools, and even more are involved in Waldorf. Part of this can be attributed through self-selection and paying fees, but a large part of parent involvement in Waldorf schools has to do with the nature of the enterprise.

Parents are simply essential for painting classrooms, preparing the playground, building sets for class plays, running the holiday fair, and serving on committees and a board of trustees. This heavy involvement of a larger percentage of the parent body means that those parents are also invested in their child's progress, participating in field trips, going to parent–teacher conferences, and helping with homework projects. Their children feel that commitment, know that their parents are sacrificing time and resources, and know that education is a family priority. Many Waldorf families sacrifice vacations, home improvements, and furnishings to place scarce dollars toward their child's education. This matters socially as well as economically. Children in such an environment feel the scaffolding of support and are more likely to study hard and struggle *through* challenges rather than run away. This builds resilience.

To summarize, character education occurs:

- when a school is also a community so that students develop inter-generational, long-term relationships;
- when interdisciplinary learning supports contextual thinking so that students learn to see the world holistically and have confidence in their own problem solving skills;
- when crafts and an emphasis on practical skills teach children a "can-do" attitude, a strong connection to the world around them, and a track record of overcoming obstacles so that they develop confidence in themselves;
- when cooperation and collaboration are valued more than competition so that Waldorf graduates enjoy working in groups and feel comfortable with team projects in a variety of future jobs;
- when exposure to Nature is not a luxury but a cherished part of the day so that children learn to discover the many wonders found in the great outdoors and develop a lifelong respect and reverence for the environment;
- when exposure to the media is strictly limited so that children can participate in health-giving alternative activities;
- when *kairos*, the right time, is honored in both child development and the curriculum so that the essential worth and dignity of the unfolding human being remains the number one priority of teachers and parents;
- when every single child is seen as a miracle that deserves the full attention and devotion of teachers so that they can unfold individually and find their own particular destiny path in life;

- when emotional and intra-personal intelligence is valued as much as other forms of knowing (Howard Gardner), so that children can find their own ways of learning in search of knowledge that can ripen over time into wisdom;
- and when parent involvement demonstrates commitment to education and helps children not only persevere but also become more resilient.

Character cannot be taught, but must be cultivated. A Waldorf school provides a rich soil from which young human beings can grow over time. Rather than assess each year and quantify learning in percentages and scores, Waldorf educators look for results that may take decades to become fully manifest. As with trees and many other living things, time is the true test of value and success. Most of the qualities described here take time to develop. Old wine and venerable trees exist due to the generosity of time. Our children deserve a character education that focuses on capacities (not just skills) that can withstand the test of time—imagination, problem solving, social sensitivity, and critical thinking. People with character, compassion, and integrity are the bedrock of a just and sustainable culture.

6

Sustainability

Teachers today face mounting pressures on all fronts:

- Parents have high expectations for academic achievement and often want to see results immediately.
- Administrators often add another layer of pressure in the name of accountability and assessment.
- Teachers sometimes feel that they are left out of crucial decisions that affect their classroom.
- Those working in independent schools fear the loss of families and enrollment, which can lead to budget cuts and in some cases the elimination of jobs/programs.
- The special needs of children today are diagnosed more readily but also present more challenges to classroom teachers; in some cases 1/3 or more of a given group of children have individualized learning needs.
- After investing time and resources in certification and professional training, teachers sometimes find that they are marginalized; school boards and administrators decide on programs and pedagogy without adequate teacher participation.

As a result of these pressures (and there are more!), teachers today often feel unprotected, exposed, and vulnerable. Some leave the profession entirely; others do not enter, and the remainder often have to hunker down and try and simply slog on. So the question arises: Is this situation sustainable?

Waldorf schools have long held to the "class teacher" model, in which one teacher leads a group of children from first to eighth grade. This has many advantages:

- Continuity of relationship with the children including follow-through on learning needs and differentiating the curriculum based on real knowledge of the individual children in the class.
- Offering a curriculum that follows child development and is truly age appropriate. Children learn more when lesson content speaks to them!
- Teachers in a Waldorf school can educate toward wholeness; a class teachers can model and demonstrate how all subjects are interrelated. So, for example, the life of Thomas Edison is not only a biography but also includes the science of his inventions and the history of his time. A truly interdisciplinary approach.
- Education is seen as an art, which means that a good teacher takes any given subject and transforms it into living, engaging lessons that enhance personal growth.
- A Waldorf teacher has to prepare new lesson content each year and thus is less likely to grow stale, sour, or cynical. Learning new material with enthusiasm can be contagious!

Yet these opportunities also add another layer of demands on the Waldorf teacher. Expectations are high. So again, the question arises: is this sustainable?

Then there are the social pressures felt by parents, teachers, and many in the helping professions: life stressors, of which there are many; loss of community spirit; drug epidemics; and more. Teachers feel a tremendous responsibility to do the right thing, to help prepare young people for a better world, yet at the same time societal pressures encroach more and more into the life of the classroom. Teachers are often expected to "fix" everything but are given fewer and fewer resources to do so. Again, is this sustainable?

To summarize by using an image from an old fairy tale, teachers are often expected to spin gold from straw. Having lived with these issues most of my professional life, and having wrestled with these and many other challenges in the teaching profession myself, I have no magic solutions. Indeed, I am cautious about any new fad or popular solution that promises to fix it all. Of course, governance structures and teacher involvement in them matter. Of course, more resources would seriously help. But, in the end, I have found that one has to begin where one can have the most immediate impact: with oneself and one's own classroom. We have countless choices still left to us, and we can optimize those opportunities at hand, and in so doing, leverage small successes into larger achievements. Every lesson, each moment of the day, we can decide *how we want to live, learn, and teach*. The crucial word is HOW. If we can find the best way possible to live, learn, and teach, we can still make a difference. The example below is meant to demonstrate how a simple instance of lesson preparation can be done as a "chore" or as a means toward resiliency.

If we have strong, resilient teachers who model health and inner wholeness, we are far more likely to have children who are inspired, knowledgeable, and emotionally intelligent. And these sorts of graduates are less likely to resort to default actions such as violence and other forms of antisocial behavior.

An example from the classroom of six-year-olds that illustrates the power of the HOW:

Assignment: Tell the story "The Lily and the Lion" to build listening skills, comprehension, vocabulary, and early reading and writing skills.

Option A: Read the story a few times, learn as much of it as possible (a Waldorf teacher is asked to tell it "by heart"), practice at home and tell the story in class in front of a roomful of children whom, one hopes, will pay attention for the duration.

Option B: Read the story over many days so it sinks in; learn it by heart and then go deeper. This involves living with the pictures, learning to see through the images, working on the riddles, and letting the story grow from within over time. Here are some examples from "The Lily and the Lion":

Part of narrative: Before setting out on a journey, the merchant, father of three daughters, was asked by his youngest, Lily, to bring her a rose upon his return.

Riddle: Why is her name Lily, why a rose, and what do they signify?

Reflections: Flowers give us joy; they speak to us in so many ways because they are expressions of the soul in physical form. It must not be a coincidence that the story features these two, the lily, and the rose. What do they represent?

In ancient traditions, the phrase "under the rose" meant to take an oath of silence so that the divine could enter the heart. Earthly senses need to be silenced for this to happen. The rose calls on us to transform the earthly into what lives in sunlight and wisdom.

Whereas the rose has thorns and demonstrates the harsh realities of the world that can lead to beauty in the blossom, the lily is a flower of annunciation. It is more juicy, fluid in movement, has leaves to the point of being mostly leaf. Thus the rose represents the hard path of life experience while the lily indicates mercy and unexpected blessing.

Application: Here, at the very beginning of the story, we have two very different soul gestures, two pathways, and two resources for the teacher with an inquiring mind:

1. How can we transform subjects, or curriculum, into experiences that speak to the children? (Rose)

2. How can we empty ourselves to receive inspirations and spiritual insight? (Lily)

3. Most of all, how can we make sure that our desire for the "perfect" does not get in the way of the possible and, especially, does not cloud our chance to work with our imperfections?

Part of narrative: Struggling to find a rose in the winter, the merchant comes across a castle with a garden, half of which is in winter and half in summer (and is thus able to get a rose). Later on, it turns out that the lion is an enchanted prince who roams the world as a lion by day and becomes a prince at night.

Riddle: What does this mean? A garden half in winter and half in summer; in the day he is a lion and in the night a prince?

Reflections: We experience the world and ourselves differently in the summer or winter, at night or in the day. Our consciousness changes. It may not be as dramatic as becoming an animal by day and human at night, but we are different in our awareness of self and others. When am I living more in the "night consciousness," asleep to some of the things going on around me? Do I strive too hard at times to be constantly in a "day consciousness"? How can working with the seasonal and daily rhythms support me?

Application: Since I am a morning person, I need to prepare adequately before sleep but leave time to harvest what often proves to be the best inspirations in the morning (such as writing books, teaching, etc.) And I have to guard against late afternoon and evening meetings when I am at half-mast and can make mistakes, be too reactive, etc.

Part of narrative: To reclaim her beloved who has now been changed into a dove, Lily has to wander the world for seven long years, led and sustained only by a white feather that he would let fall once a day.

Riddle: Why seven years? Why a white feather from a dove?

Reflections: Our physical body, cells and all, is renewed every seven years. We also experience seven-year cycles in human biography. Seven speaks to completion and renewal. The white feather from a dove is a sign of hope and our best wishes for a better future. We endure because we have hopes and dreams. A dove can represent the purification of desires and an overcoming of enchantment/illusions/falsehood. Our striving (journey) over time (seven years), trial and error can lead us to our higher, ideal selves (dove).

Application: Why am I teaching? Do I have a chance to renew my connection to the ideals that started me on the journey? Do those ideals still have merit and are they still able to awaken creative forces within me?

The examples from "The Lily and the Lion" are just one opportunity to move from option A to option B; from a task to a place of fulfillment. Ironically, the latter happens even if we do not arrive at any final answers. It is the asking of questions, the living with the riddles, that serves to nourish and sustain. There are countless other opportunities that could be cited, some with amazing parallel narratives. For instance, in both fifth and tenth grades, Waldorf students work with Homer's *Odyssey*. Here again, we have the journey, striving, and the self-education of a human being. Homer presents us with many riddles, most of which we will never solve. But the inner engagement of the teacher will make those lessons ever so alive and fulfilling.

Thus, the answer to the repeated question on sustainability has to do with HOW, more than what or even when. A good teacher can use practically any material to draw forth learning. It is helpful when there is a sense of timing (when), especially in regard to child development (*The Odyssey* works well in tenth, but would most likely bomb in ninth). But in terms of building resiliency in both teacher and student, the how is the key.

More than ever before, our schools need to think less of test scores and verifiable outcomes and more about building resilience. Much of the material in this book is dedicated to that end. No one has ever asked me about my SAT test scores in the many years since I took them. But who I am as a human being, my ability to draw forth meaning and understand life experiences, my ability to relate to others and communicate are front and central every day at work and at home. Thus, teaching with the HOW leads in the end to WHO. Who you are as a person is the crucial difference. To strive toward a less violent society, we need more attention to this crucial ingredient in every equation of life: the human being.

Does this lesson speak to our humanity? Does it enhance respect for others and support human dignity? Is there material, whether in science, math, history, or English that can grow over time, or is it presented as dead end, dry facts that are soon forgotten? Are we nourishing the soul or just taxing the mind? Can we strive to teach out of wholeness, a view of the complete human being that is multi-faceted, complex, and inherently mysterious? Finally, as indicated in the last chapter of this book, do children have rights to a complete and comprehensive education regardless of zip code or family of origin?

I hope we can all become advocates of a children's Bill of Rights, one that is just as fundamental to our survival as is the one attached to our constitution. The time for debate is over. The time for focused advocacy, for the basic educational rights of all children, is at hand.

In addition to the classroom and self-care, there is one major initiative I would like to urge on all schools, especially independent Waldorf schools that have been in existence for some time: We need to do much, much more to connect with alumni. At a recent AWSNA conference in March 2017, I asked the 110 participants from twenty schools to figure out how many students they have graduated over the years. Since most schools represented at the conference were from the New England region, and many of those schools have been serving children for many years, I suggested the total for all schools in the region must be quite high. Then I asked them to remember how successful most of their alums have been, the career paths they have followed, and their many achievements. Then came the imagination: Suppose we were able to network and communicate with all those alums in the region? Imagine we could tap into their expertise and goodwill? Then, through a process of collaboration and shared interests (of which Waldorf would certainly be a high priority), imagine each alum were to make a yearly donation to our regional association to support schools according to their ability to give? Then came the closer: I firmly believe that if the above were to happen, we could collectively declare our schools tuition free!

Parents would of course still need to pay fees for supplies, extracurricular events etc. But for the most part their efforts could go toward finding new families and helping build the future through new buildings and programs. In short, we would enter a virtuous cycle in which the yearly operating budget would be covered through the regional association and the parent/friend work would build the future. The stronger schools would in turn attract more families, and more students would graduate each year thus increasing the alum base.

With the foregoing paragraphs, I wish to suggest that we need to address financial sustainability in new and bolder ways. We need to broaden our community base as well as deepen the pedagogy. With depth and breadth we then have the intersection of spiritual and material resources. The horizontal and vertical work, when done with integrity and passion, can then yield a "bonus," a third element that is a gift from the spiritual worlds. This third element is a matter of serendipity, or the unexpected. Someone walks in the door of the school and writes an article as a result of the experience, a grandparent leaves a sizable legacy, or a Waldorf book becomes a bestseller! One way to picture this third element is to picture the Irish cross, which has a circle around the central intersection: ✞. Reaching out, reaching in, and awaiting the circling of good spirits that want our children to be well educated...this is an imagination of sustainability.

7

BOYS

Many of the chapters in this book focus on the spiritual and pedagogical issues needing our attention if we are to build a less violent world. One could say that my overall approach, as with Waldorf education in general, is proactive. Yet there is also a need to look at some of the harsh realities of growing up in today's world, issues such as antisocial behavior, juvenile violence, addictions, and mis-education. These issues cry out for much more attention and research than I can give it in the context of this book, so I decided to focus mostly on one crucial element in the equation: boys. Often seen as "the problem" from ordinary classroom management perspectives to incarceration rates, boys need to be understood and engaged as never before. My goal with this section is to elevate a few issues in the hope that schools will take them up in active discussion, parents will self-reflect, and some of our mental images will begin to change. I will begin with a few facts on risk factors, the juvenile justice system in relation to boys and girls, insights from an author I discovered while in New Zealand, and end with some of Rudolf Steiner's advice on adolescence.

Following are five factors that can contribute to teen violence:

1. *Mental Health Issues*

Teens who respond with violence and harsh words may be struggling with any number of mental health issues. ADD/

ADHD, anxiety, depression, bipolar, and more can trigger negative behavior that includes violence. If teen boys have not been getting any kind of emotional or mental health assistance from trained and licensed professional, the violent behavior usually escalates. Intensive group and individual therapy can help teens with any number of disorders and conditions that can leave them feeling frustrated and unable to cope.

2. *Trauma*

It is often difficult for teenagers to cope with trauma in their lives, such as physical or sexual abuse, adoption and abandonment issues, post-traumatic stress, and similar events. Teens often are not able to process what has happened to them without counseling and professional therapy, and so they act out in violent ways to communicate their hurt, fear, and anger.

3. *Home Life*

Teens that come from a dysfunctional home, where parents wield very harsh or very lax discipline practices, are more likely to become violent themselves. Domestic-abuse situations can further demonstrate to teens that the only way to handle conflict is through physical intimidation. Other family influences toward violence include poverty, low education, low community involvement, and low parental involvement in the teenage boy's life.

4. *Community Influence*

Where a teenager lives can have an impact on their behavior, positive or negative. Socioeconomically disadvantaged neighborhoods and cities can directly influence a community culture that accepts and even encourages violence. Many areas are full of crime and gang activity, which can heighten a teenage boy's need to act violently. Poverty, neighborhood downturn, lots of unsupervised teens, increased presence in drugs and guns, and other conditions can lead to teens that are more violent.

5. Delinquent Friends

Teen boys who hang around delinquent social groups are also more likely to get involved in violence. Gang activity or other teen groups who regularly get in trouble with the law boost a teenage boy's chances of becoming violent. Often, teenagers who join up with a group of friends that abuse drugs and alcohol regularly will likely increase their violent behavior.

※

Parents, teachers, and community members should all look at the factors that contribute to teen violence and take the necessary steps to intervene in each teenage boy's life and help him avoid or overcome violent behavior.*

When we look at Waldorf schools in general, most parents would affirm that there is a strong emphasis on community life and supporting home life through the festivals, assemblies, shared values such as the importance of storytelling, bedtime, outdoor education, and so on. These are present in urban settings and in small rural schools. Likewise, as a byproduct of staying with one group over many years and the continuity of relationships, it is less likely that Waldorf children will hang out with delinquent friends. Of course, Waldorf schools in themselves cannot prevent mental health issues or the occurrence of traumatic events in a child's life; tragedy and struggle come to many, regardless of economic status or schooling. Yet there is a strong current of caring and therapeutic insight within the faculty of most Waldorf schools I have visited. In some cases, schools even bring in art

---

*   Liahona Academy, http://www.liahonaacademy.com/contributing-factors-to-teen-boys-with-violent-behavior.html (accessed July 22, 2017).

therapists and/or have care groups that tend to special situations. Many schools contend with limited resources of time, expertise, and/or finances, but most parents would agree that the pedagogy in itself is healing. The arts of drama, painting, singing, speech, and eurythmy develop emotional intelligence and allow for contained processing of some of the challenges life brings. But most of all, the heart forces of Waldorf teachers ray out and nourish the inner lives of the children in their care. Simply put, Waldorf students are loved, and as Rumi said so well, love conquers all.

Now to bring another perspective to the topics covered in this book, here are some interesting facts concerning girls and boys in the juvenile justice system: While girls have historically made up a small percentage of the juvenile justice population, offending by girls is on the rise. Not only is the overall number of juvenile delinquency cases for nonviolent crimes on the rise, girls are accounting for a larger proportion of the delinquency pie than they did during the 1980s. While violent crime by juveniles has decreased overall since 1985, girls are committing more of those offenses than they did in 1985.

- Between 1980 and 2003, youth arrests increased—peaking in the mid-1990s—and then decreased. Because female arrests increased more sharply and then fell more gradually, the share of female juvenile arrests grew from twenty to twenty-nine percent in those years.
- Between 1985 and 2002, the overall number of delinquency cases for girls increased ninety-two percent—as opposed to a twenty-nine percent increase for boys. Some of these increases are certainly due to a rise in female offending, but some may also be due to the fact that offending girls once treated with kid gloves by the justice system are now receiving the same attention as the boys.

- While most offenses that lead to arrest are committed by boys, girls account for the majority of arrests for certain types of offenses such as running away—fifty-nine percent—and prostitution and commercialized vice—sixty-nine percent.
- Female offenders are *less* likely than male offenders to be arrested and formally charged for most offenses. Once charged, however, female offenders are *more* likely than male offenders to receive secure confinement.
- Research suggests that girls may be becoming more violent—over the past several decades the share of arrests for aggravated assault by girls increased from fifteen percent to twenty-four percent of total arrests. This increase may be due in part to an increase in violent behavior by girls, but it might also be due in part to changes in policy, such as the reclassification of simple assault into aggravated assault.
- In 1980, boys were four times as likely as girls to be arrested for a violent crime; today they are only twice as likely. This is partly explained by the fact that while *all* violent crime has decreased, the decline for boys has been more dramatic. For example, the female share for violent crimes such as robbery and murder remained relatively stable from 1980 to 2003. Moreover, girls account for a very small proportion of some of the most serious types of crimes—such as homicide and sexual assault.
- In detention, the pattern of violent behavior reverses: research shows that female juvenile offenders are more violent toward staff in institutionalized settings than male offenders.
- Boys and girls generally start offending at the same ages for less serious types of crime (e.g., drug offenses), but for more serious or violent types of crime, girls tend to start offending at a *younger* age than boys.

- Female youth offenders have higher rates of mental illness than male youth offenders. In the general population, girls have higher rates of what are termed "internalizing" mental disorders (e.g., depression and anxiety) while boys have higher rates of "externalizing" disorders (e.g., ADHD, conduct disorder, and other behavioral problems). Among juvenile justice populations, however, girls exhibit higher rates of *both* types of mental disorders, as well as a greater number of overall symptoms of mental illness than is usually seen in the general population.

Assessment and Treatment

Most assessment tools and treatment models used with youth in the justice system were designed for use with male offenders and have not been adequately tested with females. Until we have more research, we cannot know if these assessments and interventions are effective with offending girls.

Given the high rates of mental health disorders of female offenders, it is imperative that services be offered. However, girls with conduct disorders are far less likely than their male counterparts to find, receive, or complete treatment. The lack of community-based treatment options for offending girls gives rise to two related problems:

- Many programs are "boys only"—i.e., they are designed specifically for boys (but are technically open to all), or do not accept girls at all.
- Programs that do accept girls do not address female-specific needs.

Long-term Consequences

Engaging in antisocial behavior has long-term negative consequences for girls that reach well into adulthood. Even if they have stopped offending, women with a history of juvenile delinquency have higher mortality rates, more mental health problems, dysfunctional and violent relationships, and poorer educational and employment outcomes than women who do not have a history of delinquency.

Both male and female juvenile offenders often exhibit negative behaviors once they reach adulthood, regardless of whether they continue to engage in criminal behavior during adulthood. However, more females express their negativity with children, romantic partners, and other family members than do males. For example:

- Marriage: For offending males, marriage and increased responsibility have a positive influence, helping them to discontinue their criminal behavior. For females, the opposite is true—female offenders are more likely to marry a mate who is also antisocial, which then leads to more drug abuse, criminal behavior, and relationship conflict.
- Domestic violence: Instead of "outgrowing" their offending behavior as the vast majority of boys do, women with histories of juvenile delinquency appear to replace their criminal behaviors with violence toward their partners. Some of this abuse is serious enough to necessitate medical treatment and create fear in the victim.
- Children: Female offenders are more likely to pass an antisocial legacy on to the next generation. Female youthful offenders tend to have children at a younger age than their non-offending counterparts—usually with a father who is also antisocial. The combination of early parenthood with

the multitude of stressors that female offenders face—such as poverty, domestic violence, and poor parenting skills—place their children at increased risk to follow in their footsteps.

Conclusion

In summation, girls in the justice system experience a multitude of risk factors, often at higher rates than their male counterparts experience. Offending girls exhibit higher rates of mental health problems, exhibit more aggression toward family members and romantic partners, and suffer more negative consequences from their justice system involvement than offending boys. Antisocial girls are less likely to access treatment and have fewer community-based treatment options than boys have, despite their increased need for services. Finally, girls who are formally charged are more likely to be placed in secure confinement than boys are in the same situation and to act out violently once there. The combination of these factors puts female offenders on a pathway to continued justice system involvement and long-term dysfunction that they carry on into adulthood and pass on to their children."[*]

Delving more into the question of raising boys, a friend introduced me to a book written by the first female prison supervisor in an all-male penitentiary in New Zealand, *He'll Be OK: Growing Gorgeous Boys into Good Men* by Celia Lashlie. She did extensive interviews with inmates, and also with principals and teachers at a variety of schools in New Zealand. Since her

---

[*] Adapted from Elizabeth Cauffman, "Understanding the Female Offender"; and Thomas Grisso "Adolescent Offenders with Mental Disorders," in *The Future of Children: Juvenile Justice*, vol. 18, no. 2, fall 2008 (http://www.jstor.org/stable/120179974); and Melissa Sickmund, "OJJDP Fact Sheet: Delinquency Cases in Juvenile Court 2005," Office of Juvenile Justice and Delinquency Prevention: June 2009 (this "highlight" was prepared by Hilary Hodgdon).

prison population was all male, she gathered first hand experiences, some of them alarming, others insightful or even humorous, about how to raise (or not raise) boys in today's world. Along the way she tested several long held assumptions about both parenting and teaching. For example, in a world that continually urges equality and maximum verbal engagement with children, she ended up making a strong case for mothers to back off when it comes to their teenage boys (not make school lunches anymore, for instance) and that they should let fathers take a stronger role in their lives, even when it means long periods of silence.

Celia's observations include the importance of boys' rites of passage, their need to know that what they are saying is important to the listener, and the positive effects of sport in their lives—for the competition, for the sense of belonging, and for their relationship with their own bodies:

> In my discussions with the boys themselves, I came to understand that, for the vast majority of the boys, sport is an integral part of the journey to manhood both because of its competitive nature and because it gives them the sense of being a part of something bigger than themselves.... Sport also means they can continue to build a positive relationship with their body and use their high energy levels and a positive way. (p. 45)

Waldorf schools have a high commitment to movement, including a regular schedule of eurythmy (frequently mentioned in this text), spatial dynamics, circle activities, and outdoor games. As a parent of six, I have to admit that many Waldorf schools have an uneven track record when it comes to organized sports. The issues regarding pros and cons of competitive sport are generally present in faculty discussions, yet in a well-intentioned effort to stress cooperative games, Waldorf schools lose boys, particularly in grades six to eight. Lashlie's points are well taken, and I feel that when boys migrate to other schools because they seek more engagement in sports, we all lose out. My view is that basketball, volleyball, baseball, and lacrosse (to name a few) are all part of a well-rounded physical education. If Spacial Dynamics®* is taught well (see literature on the field by Jaimen McMillan), and if the school is fortunate enough to have a eurythmy program, then there can also be room in the lives of both boys and girls for organized sports.

My youngest son, Ionas, has been passionate about lacrosse and basketball, which have helped build his physical and emotional stamina, and his coaches have often played a formative role in his life, bringing lessons that go beyond the particular sport. All schools need to offer a balanced physical education program.

Lashlie urges us all to give boys the precious gift of time—time to process newfound emotions and make decisions about their future. In her discussions with students, she began to understand that boys are guided by pragmatism, intuition, and living in the moment, they probably need a few big challenges and not many baby steps, and they tend to get tunnel vision on whatever the end goal may be. She addresses an aspect that leads straight to the risks mentioned earlier in this chapter, which is that boys do not really feel they have any control over their lives. So while they are aware of the consequences of their choices, they do not feel that their decisions have any real impact (p. 59). "We women seem to move in the circle, expanding its edges as we move and drawing in more and more 'stuff'. Men move in a straight line, often ignored everything that off to the sides as they focus on what needs to be done" (p. 59).

---

* Cf. https://www.spacialdynamics.com/.

Lashlie affirms that again and again boys have shown her, both in action and word, that they live mostly in the moment, which is why learning impulse control is so important. And there are some deep-seated attitudes toward schools that affect boys:

> On a number of occasions, I gained the impression that they felt the world was stacked against them: girls were perceived to be better students because they were tidier in their work and paid more attention to detail, and the external world favored women over men.... There's a fine line between the perception that girls learn differently from boys and the perception that they learn better. The boys often appeared to be receiving the latter message.... As discussions continued, I began to connect their fear of failure not only to their desires to live in the moment, but also too their unwillingness to plan....
>
> A regular topic of discussion was the management and processing of emotions. As we talked it became apparent that the only real acceptable emotion adolescence boys feel able to display is anger. Any other potentially negative emotion, such as grief, hurt or sadness, is transmuted into anger and dealt with accordingly.... They were adamant that talking doesn't generally help and couldn't be persuaded otherwise. (p. 61–64)

Then, in a series of bulleted statements, Lashlie outlines a few key points that are valid for all parents and teachers: The central issue in the lives of adolescent boys is getting mother off the bridge of adolescence, and fathers onto it (p. 94).

- Alcohol is about easing the pressure of moving toward manhood, about finding common ground with their peers and girls, and simply about having fun.
- As soon as we lower the drinking age we put adolescent boys at significantly higher levels of risk.
- Adolescent girls are matching or even surpassing adolescent boys in the tendency to sometimes get extremely drunk.

- With regard to drugs, the hypocrisy of adults doesn't go unnoticed.
- Keeping boys busy in years nine, ten, and eleven allows time for anti-drug messages to sink in.
- Sport is an integral part of the journey to manhood for the vast majority of boys.
- Most boys believe that women are in charge.
- The challenge is how to use the pragmatism of adolescent boys in a way that supports their development and helps mothers in particular to stop expending energy on trying to make their sons into something they are not.
- To connect with him and encourage him in making good decisions, we need to step into his time frame.
- Adolescent boys have to be able to see and/or feel the consequences of doing or not doing something before it becomes real enough to matter and to motivate them.
- The pragmatic lens through which an adolescent boy looks is very narrow and has room only for himself. The pragmatic lens through which a mature adult man looks can incorporate the idea of doing things for others.
- Women need to accept the reality of men rather than forever wanting to change it and them. (pp. 126-127)
- Mothers, particularly white middle-class mothers, are overly involved in the lives of their adolescent sons.
- Men's business at this point in the lives of boys is to guide them through adolescence. Women's job is to step back.
- It will be his intuition that keeps him safe, keeps him from making dumb decisions, and you can help him to develop it.
- When we push information into boys heads before they are thirteen, that information will eventually reemerge in unexpected ways, often as raw emotion. We need to teach in a

way that students can process, not just to store information for the next test.
- If your son is now a secondary school student and you're still making his lunch, please seriously consider stopping.
- By interfering in the process, women are not allowing our boys to learn about action and consequences. We must not do this if they are to have any chance of successful and enjoyable lives. (pp. 165–166)

Then she goes on to talk more about men and communication in general:

> I'm now convinced that, in general, about eighty percent of men's communication is silent and if men are communicating with other men, that ratio rises above ninety percent. They communicate with hand gestures, with their eyes and eyebrows, with their head, and then and only then do they speak. In complete contrast to women, they do not talk unless there's something to say....
>
> Men are highly intuitive; they appeared to use their intuition as a communication tool with considerable success. The challenge for women is to recognize the communication that is occurring in silence and trust it, let it be, rather than insisting that everything be openly discussed.
>
> I've often reflected on what I might have done differently with my son during his adolescents had I known then what I know about the power of male intuition and the way it develops. I think the answer is that I would have to talk to his intuition rather than to his belligerence....
>
> It seems to me there's a tendency in society at the moment to assume that views expressed by women are right until proven wrong and that those expressed by men a wrong until proven right. I don't want it to be so and I was keen to take part in Good Man Project partly to prove this idea wrong. Unfortunately the project didn't do that; rather it added considerable weight to my impression that this is exactly how things stand. As a result, the project, and this book, became focused on getting women to step back as they approached

the bridge of adolescence with their son and allow room for his father to come forward; to be quiet at times and note the conversations that are actually occurring between men and boys; to see the inherent beauty and strength and men when they're allowed to be themselves rather than the sort of men we think we want them to be. (pp. 134–181)

Lashlie also has a comment that will sound familiar to many teachers who have participated in parent conferences:

> I've talked about the situation when two parents are called in to discuss their son with the principal and the mother does all the talking. The father obviously has something to say, but can't get it out because the mother won't stop talking long enough for him to get his thoughts organized. When I put this to a group of men, they explain that they don't speak because they're afraid of getting it wrong (p. 186).

Finally, Lashlie sums up the three qualities of a good man as trust, loyalty, and a sense of humor. She emphasizes the extraordinary importance of role models for boys:

> In our discussions they identified three distinct groups of men, each of whom acted as a role models for them in different ways. There was a man who had access to what the students might want in later life (wealth, cars, power); the man who had achieved excellence in their particular field of interest; and the men they might actually want to be like.... That is what led me on the third category, which I'm inclined to call heroes. These were the men they knew personally, the men they actually aspire to be like. In this group there were grandfathers, uncles, their older brothers and their mates' older brothers, their teachers and their coaches and, on a rare occasion, their fathers. It's here rather than in the public arena that we should be looking for potential positive male role models. (pp. 200–201).

These positive role models are not so easy to come by in today's world. Star athletes are exposed for drug use, pop stars die of overdoses, and fathers and uncles are often at a distance. And the media and movie industry often conspire to project images of men as bumbling fools. In sitcoms, for example, men are often portrayed as incompetent and easily manipulated by the women in their lives. This has an effect on teenage boys. We recently went to see an inspiring documentary on women in Peru who were brought into a cottage industry making dolls. It was a moving story, but halfway through I started to look at the documentary through the eyes of my fifteen-year-old son sitting next to me. The husbands in the film were either nonexistent or portrayed as abusive—even the male founder of the enterprise. I understand the film was about Peruvian women, but when we were driving home afterward I initiated a conversation with my son on what we had experienced. I will not recount that father/son conversation here (and there were many silences!), but toward the end I felt impelled to talk more about the founder and the many other men in the world who are also doing good work on behalf of social justice. I felt he needed to hear that from me.

For these are no small matters. Boys need their father, uncles, coaches, and other positive role models:

> But I now believe that the real answers to such problems as youth suicide, youth offending and imprisonment and the increasing youth road toll lies in strengthening boys' links to the good men and their immediate circle, their heroes, and in helping fathers to remain heroes and positive influences in the lives of their sons.
>
> The answer also lies in getting ordinary men's stories into the cultural fabric of our society. During the project I spent an evening with the principals involved during which each of them spoke for five to ten minutes, sharing their stories of when they had become men. It will remain one of the most memorable nights of my life. To watch adult men reach back to find that moment and then find the words to share it with peers was to know the strength, humor, and

pure delight of men when they're affirmed for being who and what they are. If men can begin to share these stories with their sons, with other men and perhaps even with their wives and partners, and if we honor those stories within our society as they deserve to be honored, we'll be taking a significant step forward in guiding our young man successfully across the bridge of adolescence into manhood. (p. 203)

In the end, the work with boys is all about building emotional confidence, "the ability to ask and answer reflective questions; the ability to think about the world around them and their part in it; and the ability to find the language to describe how they see that world" (p 206). Boys do have things to say, but they often lack the vocabulary and the confidence to say what they are thinking.

The following are observations from the perspective of a Waldorf high school.

A materialistic view of the human being leads to earthbound hardening of the human being and a tendency toward physical solutions to interpersonal and human challenges. One could say that violence is a gravitational force that hardens positions further and splinters a community. Simplistic, outer cause and effect views of problem solving can give rise to crude, physical solutions to real needs and issues. One way to counteract this is through the methods we employ in teaching.

When we serve children readymade conclusions and abstract theories, we are pushing down a learning process into the limbs and feet of our students. It is made even worse when one then tests everything, forcing children to cram and then forget. In contrast, teaching as an art involves inviting children to explore in imagination, and real experiences, the many aspects of a lesson, and then gradually form their own judgments that weigh and consider the lesson over several days. Only then should conclusions be invited. So for instance, in teaching geometry in 8th grade, we did a unit on the Platonic solids. The children heard the life of Plato, crafted the solids in clay, and then made mobile out of colorful construction paper. We then looked at the surfaces and points and began to consider their relationships. Only after a few days did we push further into ratios and thus draw some conclusions. The students were engaged and active in thinking, feeling, and willing which also addressed the various learning styles and needs of my students in ways that I could not have fully anticipated.

Abstract theory followed by testing is a kind of soul violence perpetrated on all too many children in our schools today. When one has a fixed mental picture or idea followed by the demand to bring it into action such as writing answers in a test, one goes straight from the conceptual into volitional activity that is not self-directed but imposed from without. A natural response is to rebel, and healthy children act out in a variety of ways. Sometimes it is overt behaviors that fall under the heading of "classroom management," sometime it is boredom and apathy. Along the way we damage their sleep life and promote disconnection from life.

> Believe me, everything we can mediate to children via feelings allow their inner life to grow, while an education that consist of mere thoughts and ideas is devoid of life, remains dead. Ideas and thoughts are no more than mirror images....
>
> If we concentrate on the recent local history at the expense of events in the distant past, if (as it were) we put the emphasis in our lesson on cultivating a wrong patriotism (you will easily think of many such instances)—then we shall greatly engender obstinacy and willfulness of the inner life and a tendency toward moodiness. These are side effects, which will, above all, make people reluctant to observe world events objectively. And this is so terrible today. Neglecting geography and taking the wrong

approach to history have greatly contributed to serious illnesses of our times.*

Inability to observe world events objectively can lead to fanaticism in political and religious views that sometime become extreme in desperate acts of violence. One could say that mis-education leads to soul imbalances which can lead to disconnection, fixed mental images, and bursts of "will activity" that hurt many people. Education today is both part of the problem and the solution to our current social crisis. In addition to the social implications, there are serious health effects of mis-education:

> If teachers become aware of these things, they will almost see that when they are reading in the wrong way, when they bore the children they will tend toward metabolic illness; teachers will feel that, by making a child read a boring piece of literature, they actually produce a diabetic in later life. They will then develop the right sense of responsibility; by continuously occupying the children with boring material, we produce diabetics. If we don't calm the release of spirit after physical exercise or a singing lesson we produce people who lose themselves and life. (ibid., p. 70)

Steiner then goes on to talk more specifically about teaching methods in regard to boys and girls:

> Certainly, boys are looking for friendship or some connection. But they also feel the need to hide their thoughts and feelings. This is characteristic of boys whose "I"-beings are connected to their astral bodies in this way. Teachers who can empathize with situations present in boys and who can meet it in a subtle, delicate way will do much to help them. It is this manner of the teacher rather than a direct, crude approach that has a beneficial effect. The boy has a certain love of withdrawal into himself....

---

* Steiner, *Education for Adolescents*, pp. 40, 57.

It is different with girls. With girls, there are delicate differences, for which it is necessary to develop a certain skill in observation. The girl's "I" is more or less absorbed by the astrality. Because of this, a girl lives less strongly in her inner being....

They accentuate their personalities, are self-assured and do not withdraw into themselves. It is natural for them to confront the world freely and unashamedly....

When a boy turns into a real lout who is easily excited, this behavior does not contradict the fact that his soul and spirit are growing pale.

This is basically the expression of a new experience for feeling that takes hold of the whole being—a feeling of shame or embarrassment. It permeates the whole being and consist of feeling: I must have something in my individual, inner life that is mine that I do not wish to share with anyone else; I must have secrets....

And the boys—aggressive behavior first, then their rudeness and mean-spiritedness during the later teenage years are really nothing more than their reluctance to show the world what they really are. Wishing to make contact, they moved clumsily, lounge about, and behave differently from what they actually are. We need to consider this—boys at this age, owing to their special constitution, behave differently from what they really are and copy other people. While the children, during the first seven years, imitate naturally, teenagers do so consciously....

All this expresses their wish to make contact with the world outside—a special characteristic of teenagers. (ibid., pp. 76–81)

One might say that those who end up turning to violence are also seeing "contact with the outside world," but in an extreme form. In the above citations, one sees how common classroom education, especially Waldorf education, can have a positive impact.

We prepare the children correctly—as we must—for their life in their twenties by recognizing the fact that the subject element connects with the astral body in an independent way. Just as the human body needs a solid bone system to prevent it from sagging, so does the astral body, with its enclosed "I," need ideals at this age if it is to develop in a healthy way. We must take this seriously. Ideals, strong concepts that are permeated with will, these we must impart into the astral body as a firm, solid support.

We can notice that boys in particular feel a strong need that is age—we have only to discover this and understand it correctly—for "everyone must choose his or her own hero to follow on the way to Mount Olympus." (ibid., p. 82)

Thus, boys in particular need good role models, clear challenges in school, physical education, and the trust and confidence of teachers and parents who are willing to give them the time to grow into adulthood. Above all, they need a wide variety of real experiences—building bridges and taking apart engines—as well as abstract theory. They need to see the purpose and reason for learning a subject. They need to develop confidence through perceptible achievement. If such needs are truly met, our boys can join with girls in building rather than destroying, in creating a future worthy of all human beings.

8

Education through the Senses

In early 2017, our family visited friends on Waiheke Island, off the coast of Auckland, New Zealand. While New Hampshire froze in subzero temperatures, we were fortunate enough to enjoy blue sky, warm air, and spectacular beaches, not to mention the kindness of a wonderful family with four children. One afternoon, after an ocean swim, I walked along the shore marveling at the assortment of clamshells that had been continually washed in by the gentle waves. One had to be careful not to step on them, especially when wading out into deeper water! Then I made a return loop, returning toward our friends along the grassy section at the edge of the sand. Suddenly I stopped in my tracks. There in front of me was a row of young people, each one glued to a mobile device. They were seemingly oblivious to wind and waves. They were not even talking to each other—just sitting and acting as if nature did not exist.

The juxtaposition of beach and mobile devices was particularly jarring that day. What was wrong with this picture? How far had they traveled only to shut out the beautiful scene in front of them? What was this doing to them?

When I eventually returned to my own screen later that day, I found the latest issue of *Waldorf Today* waiting for me. It featured an interview with Sherry Turkle about her latest book:

Reclaiming Conversation: The Power of Talk in the Digital Age is a call to arms to arrest what she sees as the damaging consequences of never being far from email or text or Twitter or Facebook, in particular the impact it has on family life, on education, on romance and on the possibilities of solitude.

Using extensive interviews and half a lifetime of research, she suggests—with references to the birth of the environmental movement in the 1960s—that we are at a "Silent Spring" moment in our infatuation with life on screens rather than life in the real world, never wholly in one or the other. She measures these effects in a breakdown of empathy between children, in the consequences of increasingly distracted family interaction and a growing need for constant stimulus. (*Waldorf Today*, Feb. 2017)

One telling quote from the article is, "Daddy, stop Googling. I want to talk to you!" No wonder there has been a breakdown in empathy and social skills in general.

Then I went back to the well-known book by Richard Louv, *Last Child in the Woods: Saving Our Children from Nature-deficit Disorder*. He makes an articulate case for reclaiming nature for our children (and ourselves). The next couple of pages highlight a few of his most compelling points:

> Within the space of a few decades, the way children understand and experience nature has changed radically. The polarity of the relationship has reversed. Today's kids are aware of the global threats to the environment—but their physical contact, their intimacy with nature, is fading. That's exactly the opposite of how it was when I was a child...
>
> Yet, at the very moment that the bond is breaking between the young and the natural world, a growing body of research links our mental, physical and spiritual health directly to our associations with nature—in positive ways. Several of these studies suggest that thoughtful exposure of youngsters to nature can even be a powerful form of therapy for attention-deficit disorders and other maladies. As one scientist puts it, we can now assume that just as children

need good nutrition and adequate sleep, they may very well need contact with nature.

Reducing that deficit—healing the broken bond between our young and nature—is in our self-interest, not only because aesthetics or justice demands it, but also because our mental, physical, and spiritual health depends upon it....

Unlike television, nature does not steal time; it amplifies it. Nature offers healing for a child living in a destructive family or neighborhood. It serves as a blank slate upon which a child draws and reinterprets the culture's fantasies. Nature inspires creativity in a child by demanding visualization and the full use of the senses. Given a chance, a child will bring the confusion of the world to the woods, wash it in the creek, turn it over to see what lives on the unseen side of that confusion. Nature can frighten a child, too, and this fright serves a purpose. In nature, a child finds freedom, fantasy, and privacy; a place distant from the adult world, a separate peace. (Louv, pp. 1–8)

When I was a child growing up in Rockland County, just outside New York City, I had a favorite hemlock tree. It was much taller than our house and, fortunately for a young climber, the branches were ideally spaced. Up I would go, higher and higher, until I had a view of all the surrounding area. Then I would sit on a particularly sturdy branch, drape my arms over another in front of me, and let the wind rock me back and forth. At times I closed my eyes and then could drink in the pungent smell of needles, bark and sap. Often I felt as though the tree and I merged into one. I knew every branch, and could alternate my perch and orientation depending on my intended outlook and the weather. That hemlock tree nourished me. It was my safe place, away for everything else in the world. It also gave me a lifelong love of trees. Everywhere I have lived I planted trees, and wherever I travel I always make new tree friends. That hemlock was my silent teacher and comforter.

> But something has changed. Now we see the emergence of what I have come to call nature-deficit disorder.... It's all this *watching,*" said a mother in Swarthmore, Pennsylvania. "We've become a more sedentary society.... Now, nature's just not *there* anymore.... Over time I came to understand some of the complexity represented by the boy who preferred electrical outlets and the poet who had lost her special spot in the woods. I also learned this: Parents, educators, other adults, institutions—the culture itself—may say one thing to children about nature's gifts, but so many of our actions and messages—especially the ones we cannot hear ourselves deliver—are different. And children hear very well. (ibid., pp. 10–14)

He goes on to give a series of examples of what he calls the criminalization of natural play:

> In Pennsylvania, three brother, ages eight, ten and twelve, spent eight months and their own money to build a tree house in their backyard. The district council ordered the boys to tear it down because they had no building permit. In Clinton, Mississippi, a family happily spent four thousand dollars to build an elaborate, two-story, Victorian-style tree house. They asked the city if a permit was necessary, and a city official said no. Five years later, the city planning and zoning department announced that the tree house must be demolished because it violated an ordinance prohibiting construction of an accessory building in front of a house....
> "We tell our kids that traditional forms of outdoor play are against the rules," says Rick. "Then we get on their backs when they sit in front of the TV—and then we tell them to go outside and play. But where? How? Join another organized sport? Some kids don't want to be organized all the time. They want to let their imaginations run; they want to see where a stream of water takes them."...
> For almost two decades, the well-known Japanese photographer Keiki Haginoya photographed children's play in the cities of Japan. In recent years, "children have disappeared so rapidly from his viewfinder that he has had to bring this chapter of his work to an end." (Louv, p. 33)

In the United States, children are spending less time playing outdoors—or in any unstructured way. From 1997 to 2003, there was a decline of fifty percent in the proportion of children nine to twelve who spent time in such outside activities as hiking, walking, fishing, beach play, and gardening, according to a study by Sandra Hofferth at the University of Maryland....

Seventy-one percent of today's, mothers said they recalled playing outdoors every day as children, but only twenty-six percent of them said their kids play outdoors daily. Surprisingly, the response did not vary a great deal between mothers living in rural and urban areas.... One U.S. researcher suggests that a generation of children is not only being raised indoors, but is also being confined to even smaller spaces....

As the nature deficit grows, another emerging body of scientific evidence indicates that direct exposure to nature is essential for physical and emotional health. For example, new studies suggest that exposure to nature may reduce the symptoms of Attention Deficit Hyperactivity Disorder (ADHD), and that it can improve all children's cognitive abilities and resistance to negative stresses and depressions...

"Those who contemplate the beauty of the Earth find reserves of strength that will endure as long as life lasts" (Rachel Carson). (ibid., p. 29-37)

When reading the following citations, the reader is encouraged to correlate what is generally known about those who do harmful things to themselves and others:

> A widening circle of researchers believes that the loss of natural habitat, or the disconnection from nature even when it is available, has enormous implications for human health and child development. They say the quality of exposure to nature affects our health at an almost cellular level....
>
> Psychotherapists have exhaustively analyzed every form of dysfunctional family and social relations, but 'dysfunctional environmental relations' does not exist even as a concept," he says. The Diagnostic and Statistical Manual "defines 'separation anxiety disorder' as 'excessive anxiety

concerning separation from home and from those to whom the individual is attached.' But no separation is more pervasive in this Age of Anxiety than our disconnection from the natural world." It's time, he says, "for an environmentally based definition of mental health." ...

In America, mental-health pioneer Dr. Benjamin Rush (a signer of the American Declaration of Independence) declared, "Digging in the soil has a creative effect on the mentally ill." Beginning in the 1870s, the Quakers' Friends Hospital in Pennsylvania used acres of natural landscape and a greenhouse as part of its treatment of mental illness. During World War II, psychiatry pioneer Carl Menninger led a horticulture therapy movement in the Veterans Administration Hospital System. In the 1950s, a wider movement emerged, one that recognized the therapeutic benefits of gardening for people with chronic illnesses. In 1955, Michigan State University awarded the first graduate degree in horticultural/occupational therapy. And in 1971, Kansas State University established the first horticultural therapy degree curriculum. (ibid., pp. 43–45)

Those with special needs who live and work in a Camphill Community experience daily the benefits of farming, weaving, baking and many other practical tasks that give nourishment, health and dignity. Founded a century ago by Karl König in Scotland, there are now Campbell communities and special schools in countries around the world.

Increasingly, there are visible links between child obesity and a variety of health issues, including sleep deprivation. We cannot just blame screen time or junk food. A sedentary lifestyle and nature deficit disorder contribute to a shocking number of overweight children. Ironically, organized sports cannot provide automatic solutions to some of the issues just named. Once again, Louv says it best:

> The physical exercise and emotional stretching that children enjoy in unorganized play is more varied and less

time-bound than is found in organized sports. Playtime—especially unstructured, imaginative, exploratory play—is increasingly recognized as an essential component of wholesome child development.... In Norway and Sweden, studies of preschool children show specific gains from playing in natural settings. The studies compared preschool children who played every day on typically flat playgrounds to children who played for the same amount of time among the trees, rocks, and uneven ground of natural play areas. Over a year's time, the children who played in natural areas tested better for motor fitness, especially in balance and agility. (ibid., pp. 48–49)

And then there are the issues of biophilia and emotional health:

> The Food and Drug Administration asked pharmaceutical companies to add explicit product labeling warning about alleged links between antidepressants and suicidal behavior and thoughts, especially among children. In 2004, data analysis by Medco Health Solutions, the nation's largest prescription benefit manager, found that between 2000 and 2003 there was a forty-nine percent increase in the use of psychotropic drugs—antipsychotics, benzodiazepines, and antidepressants. For the first time, spending on such drugs, if medications for attention disorder are included, surpassed spending on antibiotics and asthma medications for children. (ibid., p. 50)

In my book, *In Search of Ethical Leadership,* I describe the role of architecture in schools in creating or hindering social and educational development. Even a classroom with a view of the outdoors can help protect children against stress.

> Children with more nature near their homes also rated themselves higher than their corresponding peers on a global measure of self-worth. "Even in a rural setting with a relative abundance of green landscape, more (nature) appears to be better when it comes to bolstering children's' resilience against stress or adversity," Wells and Evans reported. (ibid., p. 51)

The Role of the Senses from a Waldorf Perspective

The primary vehicle for experiences in nature is through the senses. They are the portals through which sights, sounds, smell, taste, and much more can enter the human being. After taking in sensory experience, the human soul holds memory pictures that can be stored for later use. Thus, even days later, we can tell our friends about a particular sunset viewed from a favorite mountaintop. Our life is richer, more complete, when we have opportunities to take in the vast array of sensory experiences from nature.

Rudolf Steiner placed sensory education as a foundational element to Waldorf education. A visit to any classroom will quickly demonstrate the breadth of sensory opportunities children have throughout a Waldorf day: singing, circle games, multiplication tables learned with a jump rope, modeling Egyptian pyramids, painting the fern in Botany, and so on. All day long, children in a Waldorf school are "fed" through the senses.

For the purposes of this chapter on personal and social health through nature, I would like to focus on two senses: touch, which most of us can relate to on a daily level, and what Steiner calls the sense of another person (their self, or "I"). First touch.

Touching something is a way of waking up to our environment. We become conscious of our boundaries through touching. We become aware, even self-conscious, as we experience ourselves as "bounded," separate from things around us (Soesman, p. 14). One could say we leave the unity of our own body when we touch something external to us. In so doing, we experience our own body in a new way. Soesman describes this return to self-experience as, "We knock on the door of the house from which we have been evicted" (p. 15). Another way of saying it is that touch releases us from the divine totality of ourselves and then we long to return to it; the tension can be tangible. When we touch something, we gain a kind of certainty, as well as the possibility of intimacy. Novalis once said, "Touching is separation and connection both at once" (Soesman, p. 17). Louv adds, "Primate studies also show that physical touch is essential to the peacemaking process" (Louv, p. 67). Touching reveals the world as a riddle. There is always more to discover. We can never get all the way inside things that are around us. As with nature, there is always more to discover!

It is interesting that a young child often says the word "I" just when it can finally touch itself all over. This new awareness of self that comes with the use of the personal pronoun points in the direction of the highest sense (Rudolf Steiner describes twelve senses (not five), of which touch is the "lowest" and the sense of the "self" of others the highest).

We know that when we hear a person speak, we do not just hear a particular sound, or even language. Even beyond the meaning imbedded in the speaking, we experience that *a particular person—she or he—*is saying something that reveals who that person is. There is a tremendous difference between one person saying something vs. another person who might even use the same words. Why is it that children will listen to one teacher and not another? Even at an early age they have an "I"-sense, a sense of *who* is speaking. And that can make all the difference. Parenthetically, as a parent I was often astonished how one of my sons would ignore some advice only to immediately agree to the same advice when uttered by one of their grandparents! The person speaking reveals *who they are* as a sum total of life experience, wisdom, and social awareness. A child listening to a grandparent or a good teacher senses the "I" in front of them; this is someone I need to listen to. Is the person speaking out of conviction, lived experience, or just for political reasons? What stands behind the ideas? Is there authenticity and sincerity? All of these things are picked up with a very particular sense of the other.

More subtly, the "I"-sense of the other reveals much as to truth. Is the person speaking truthfully or not? One can do a so called "fact check," but there is often a more immediate read of a person's truthfulness that occurs intuitively in the moment. The media and our current political discourse have threatened this ability to discern the truth of what another person is saying. As one colleague recently said, "It is almost as if people today have been anesthetized through a torrent of media stories and falsehoods to the point where many can no longer make sense of the thread of truth in a current event." Our sense of truth has been numbed and, along the way, our trust in our "I"-sense has been damaged.

How can we begin to reclaim this lost ground? Albert Soesman suggests an exercise in which one tries, at least for a few minutes, to ignore the sounds and even the language another person is using when speaking. Even more difficult, one needs to try to ignore the meaning of that person's words. Then, according to the exercise, one tries to become sensitive as to whether he or she stands behind what is being said or is insincere. This kind of listening *through* what is said is a powerful exercise that can gradually begin to reclaim the sense of the other before us. We surrender to the other. That process conjures up resistance, sympathy, antipathy, and sympathy in a wild succession of hurdles. But in the end, it is possible to emerge with a new, heightened ability to *perceive the other*. Then we have a new basis for judgment: not superficial, transitory, media fed judgments, but one that is earned through intense inner work in clearing the pathways to new perception of the other.

In terms of social relations, it is interesting that when we agree with someone, we can sit back and nurse our own ideas, elaborate, and feel comfortable in oneself. But when there is disagreement or even conflict, it is then that we meet the "I" of the other person!

By the way, I have found that the sense of the other person comes through even when the person is no longer on Earth—for example, Scott Joplin and Mozart. It is not just more music; it is also the person behind it. The same is true of the art of Picasso or Rembrandt. We can know something of the "I" of a creative genius, and thus senses such as hearing and seeing also communicate to us in connection with the sense of the other person.

In terms of connecting the foregoing descriptions of the senses of touch and "I," they are both related to boundaries—in touch, the experience of one's own boundaries; in the "I"-sense, breaking through a boundary to the other person by a new perception (also connected to sports in the chapter on boys). Experiences of boundaries are intimately connected on many levels. Tactile experiences of being in nature can develop the human capacity to sense the being of another person. Putting one's arms around a giant tree in Muir Woods in Mill Valley, California, stretching with the help of others to reach around an ancient tree is more than a fun activity. The bark is literally in your face; the smells are direct; and the separation of self and an enormous tree is an impermeable boundary regardless of how hard we try. Touching, as well as smelling, listening, seeing, and so on in nature leads to the transformation of experience that affects the "higher senses" of hearing, language, concept, and "I" (see table of the twelve senses in the appendix). The nature experiences of young children provide a social foundation for later schooling and adulthood.

If we want education that fosters peace and collaboration among human beings on Earth, we need to attend as never before to the lower senses of touch, life, movement, and balance as these can be experienced in nature and in experiential classrooms. The outer world tends to become inner and the basis of much learning throughout life.

Now let's take the case of a person who performs an act of violence, as is so often represented in the news these days. This can be inflicted on others, as in a mass shooting, or on oneself, as in suicide or a drug overdose. I would like to make the case that, in many instances, those who take this downward path experienced sensory deprivation during childhood. Addiction counselors and those who work in crisis centers could substantiate this assertion with specific examples, but even without them the reader can simply use sound common sense in determining the truth (or absence thereof) in the above statement. One can read stories of those who commit acts of aggression toward themselves or others and, in the narrative, read between the lines for any description of the crucial early years of childhood: Was this person held, kept warm, loved, and exposed to nature and music? So often, the misery of early years screams "deficit." We deprive children of the basics of sensory education at our peril. Thus, it is inspiring to visit a place such as Sophia's Hearth (an early childhood center in Keene, New Hampshire), which exemplifies the sensory-rich, nourishing environment in the early years that our world so desperately needs today.

Finally, I would like to point out one more reason for sensory education through nature and experiential classrooms: It is human nature to have desires. They lead us to many wonderful experiences. However, if unchecked, they can lead to extremes such as overeating, anger, and abuse. One of the best ways to temper the inner surge of desire is to encounter sensory experience. The portal of the senses serves as a kind of gateway that arbitrates between the inner and the outer. Desires seek to flow outward based on purely inner dynamics, whereas sense experiences flow inward. Where the two meet, one can have a kind of reality check. So one can say that the senses continually educate us and bring us a more objective reality than just our own feelings and inclinations.

For a more peaceful society, we need to strive for an education that helps children develop a new intelligence—that of self-correction and self-mastery. No teacher or book can have greater value than this timeless capacity to self-reflect, correct, and learn from life. Computer programs and curriculum packages may come and go, but the ability to transform experiences and turn them into life lessons will always be needed. Nature, sensory experience, and self-education can give our children the future they truly deserve.

9

Inclusive Recreation: Play

In May 2017, Joan Almon, a long-time leader of the Alliance for Childhood, gave a keynote talk at Antioch University New England on the importance of play. Using examples from her experience as an educator and consultant, she described how children can flourish when given opportunities for freedom in play. This chapter is possible thanks to Joan and her lifelong study of this vital topic.*

Play is a deeply rooted activity that has been well studied in human beings, especially children, and animals. In human beings the urge to play lasts throughout one's life as has been described by the anthropologist Ashley Montagu. He likens the exploration and curiosity fostered by play to the "what if" of the scientist in the laboratory. "What if I try it this way?" asks the scientist in the laboratory. Children do the same in their exploration of life, but we call it play.**

Children have a strong urge to play and use every occasion for play. Parents of playful children often "complain" that their children want to play from morning to night. They play when they're getting dressed, when they're eating, when traveling and especially during unstructured free time.

Play arises from within and is intrinsically motivated in contrast to adult work which is generally motivated by outer

---

*   Cf. Montagu, *Growing Young*.
** Much of this chapter is based (with permission) on a previously published article; see Burkhour and Almon in the bibliography for details.

needs—the need for a meal to be prepared, a roof to be repaired or a salary to be earned. Although people often describe play as "children's work" this can lead to confusion if we attribute external motivation to play. We begin to think that play is important because it leads towards a concrete goal. This is unfortunately how play is often viewed today. Play does lead to many positive outcomes, but they are not the reason children play. They play to satisfy a deep inner urge or drive, just as they eat, drink, and sleep. All lead to important outcomes, but human beings exercise them to satisfy an immediate need. Play is the same and, like eating, drinking and sleeping, it is fundamental to a healthy life.

What is Play?

Defining play is like capturing water in your hand. You have it for a moment and then it flows away. Play is elusive. When you see it or experience it you recognize it as play, yet it is hard to grasp or define. It's been said that defining play is as difficult as defining love. These are basic attributes of life and they are too vast to be contained in a simple definition.

While it can't be defined it can be described and a good description is provided by the "playworkers" in the British Isles. Playworkers support children's play and are deeply knowledgeable about it. They say: Play is a set of behaviors that are freely chosen, personally directed, and intrinsically motivated. This means that children choose what they want to play and direct it themselves, and that the motivation to do so comes from within themselves rather than externally from adults.

This description sets play somewhat apart from video games, organized sports, and other rules-based games. For instance, in the world of sports, which also has value for children, there is a difference between adult-organized games and those games children themselves organize in vacant lots of their neighborhoods.

Children initiated sandlot baseball, for instance, and they set the rules, adapting them endlessly to the immediate situation. Today's sport programs are related but are significantly different in that they are adult-run and use set rules that the children did not create or adapt.

Video games, which are frequently considered to be a new form of play, have too much input from the programmers to be considered genuine play. Adults have created the story line and, although children can adjust it, they are not in charge of it as they are when they create a game from scratch. The situation is similar with board games, card games, and other rules-based games. If the children are free to change the rules it becomes very playful. Otherwise, it may be a good activity in its own right, but it is different from child-initiated play and should not be confused with it.

In today's world when children do initiate their own play they are rarely left alone to follow it all the way through. Adults often feel the children will get more from it if the adult builds on the child's ideas and provides new information. Play becomes another means of teaching children. Adults usually do not recognize that when it comes to play, children have a genius for knowing what they need. An adult may be able to add a light touch to the child' play, but anything more than that and it becomes the adult's play rather than the child's.

Yet, adults do have a necessary role in children's play, though it is usually an invisible one. One reason that children were free to play for hours outdoors on their own in the past is that their parents were at home, usually mothers, who kept their eyes and ears open for the sounds of play, not only those of their own children, but also the sounds of the neighborhood children. A network of safety surrounded those children.

In today's world, play has largely disappeared, in part, because parents don't feel free to let children out on their own. Yet it is possible to provide a similar invisible network of safety so that children can again have a chance to play on their own. This can happen when staff is trained to create safe but adventuresome areas for play in parks and zoos, in after-school programs, on school playgrounds, in camps, and a host of other places where children gather for fun and recreation. Organized sports themselves can be made much more playful as one ice hockey coach learned when he gave the children time to organize their own game at the end of each coaching session. The coaches left the ice and the children took over in the same way he and his friends had done on the rivers and lakes of Chicago.

Playworkers in the U.K. provide a good model. They study play intensively and learn to create play environments that allow for all types of play. They create safe play environments for children but allow as much risk-taking as they feel the children can handle. They then don a cloak of invisibility and stay outside the play as much as possible so that the children can initiate and direct their own play. They do intervene when necessary and give assistance, but the emphasis is always on children taking the lead in play. In the case of children with severe disabilities they may play with the children one-on-one if that is needed. They are firmly committed to the idea that every child has a deep need to play and this has to be satisfied if the child is to develop in a healthy and wholesome way.

Park districts, zoos, children's museums, and other playful venues in North America have become very interested in the "playwork" approach for their staff, and workshops and courses are being developed across the country.

Creating safe but adventuresome play spaces for children is a challenge. One needs to comply with state standards for safety and at the same time give children opportunities for risk. Play is an ever-evolving process in which children develop new capacities by confronting difficulties. If the play arena is over-simplified, the children grow bored with it or take extreme risks such as jumping off the top of a swing set. Most American playgrounds are designed to be as risk-free as possible for fear of accidents and litigation. In Europe, a different approach is taken and there are many "adventure playgrounds" where challenges abound, where children play with "loose parts", simple play materials that can be used in dozens of different ways, to create their own environments, and in many cases where hammers, nails and other tools are available for building huts and clubhouses. Such a "hammer and nails" playground exists in Berkeley and has had a very low accident rate for over twenty years.

The Los Angeles area has two adventure playgrounds with loose parts and staff, so there is a total of three such playgrounds in the U.S. By contrast, London has eighty adventure playgrounds staffed with playworkers, and there are hundreds more throughout the British Isles, on the European continent, and in Japan.

In London, the Chelsea Adventure Playground specializes in serving children with disabilities, along with their siblings and peers. It does not seem as though hammers and nails would be appropriate for the population it serves; instead, it offers cloth and other materials with which children can build and rebuild their environment.

It is not only children who are players. Adults are as well, although they are more likely to turn to rules-based play such as golf or other sports or hobbies rather than engaging in unstructured play. When they are given a chance to engage in creative play again, most adults are astonished to find that their playful spirit is alive and well, albeit somewhat inhibited at first compared to children who play with relish and abandonment.

Increasingly, adults are asking: What about us—how can we return to unstructured play? David Hawkins and Karen Payne, who are developing Wild Zones in California and elsewhere, offer one answer. These are described as "places where adults, children and adolescents can playfully co-create new forms of public space that enliven people's connection with each other and with nature.... They differ from parks and nature reserves because they offer opportunities to alter the environment rather than leaving it untouched—places to build dens and forts and treehouses, make new pathways, mess around with water and mud, climb trees, create sculptures from natural materials, stage performances, invent games and other types of free play."[*]

The movement to restore play is growing, and it is important that it be an inclusive movement that brings together people of all ages, genders, races, ethnic, and linguistic backgrounds and abilities. In the world of play, everyone is a player and differences that may matter elsewhere soon disappear. One sees this clearly when children with different languages play together. They utilize an unspoken language of play that is more fundamental than their different tongues.

Types of Play

Children engage in many types of play, even within a single play session. A group of children may be stalking through the woods with bows and arrows. They imagine themselves to be hunters tracking game. They are engaging in imaginative and large-motor play; they are developing small-motor proficiency as they aim, point, and use their tools; they are speaking and

---

[*] Cf. http://www.wild-zone.net/ (accessed July 4, 2017).

negotiating with one another; and they are observing nature and blending with it. They are also developing practical skills for life—in this case hunting, tracking, finding their way in the woods, and much more.

Similarly, when children play house, there is imaginative play taking place, a great deal of social interaction and negotiation over roles, and skill building as they bake, sew, build their houses, and rearrange them as needed.

Keeping the play types in mind helps one better observe play and make sense of the ever-changing scenarios the children create. Keeping the types in mind is also important when setting up a playground. Most modern playgrounds encourage large-motor skills though climbing, sliding, and swinging, but children also need opportunities to play with and manipulate small parts and engage in imaginative play and other free activities.

Different types of play help children develop physical skills including strength, dexterity and eye–hand coordination, social capacities, self-knowledge and self-control, creativity, imagination and intellectual growth, and much more. There are many ways to divide play into types, but some of the main play types can be described as follows:

> **Large-motor Play:** Children love to climb, run, slide, swing, jump, and engage in every type of movement possible. They develop coordination and balance and a sense of their body in the space around them.
>
> **Small-motor Play:** This is also called manipulative play and describes play with small objects such as sticks, stones, blocks and small toys such as people, animals, and cars. Children enjoy playing with small objects and building miniature scenes. They also like stringing beads, playing with puzzles and sorting objects into types. Through such play they develop small-motor dexterity.

Mastery Play: Children will often repeat an action in play over and over until they master it. This can be small-motor, such as a little girl who taught herself to tie a bow by pretending she was going to a birthday party. In the course of a weekend she made up fifty or sixty little birthday packages with scrap paper and yarn until at last she could tie a perfect bow. Children will also practice large-motor movements until they have perfected them, such as a group of six year old boys who pretended they were in a circus and did the high wire act by walking on a narrow plank suspended between two tables. They crossed it many times, first with help from an adult and then independently, until at last they could walk it forwards and backwards, hop across it and walk it with their eyes closed.

Rules-based Play: Elementary-age children like to make up their own rules for games, but they also enjoy changing them to fit the situation. Sports and traditional games such as marbles, jacks, hopscotch, and pick-up sticks have rules, but as long as the children are organizing the games the rules are treated flexibly. When observing children one often feels that negotiating the rules is half the fun of the game. Setting rules and changing them helps children develop social skills and the ability to negotiate. They learn to express their own point of view and find ways to combine that with the views of others.

Construction Play: Building is one of the most basic forms of play that children engage in. They love to build houses and forts as well as rockets, ships, trains and every structure they can think of. They build with any material at hand: blocks, cardboard boxes, tree stumps, sticks or stones. At home they will frequently build with sofa cushions and an old sheet. Children need loose parts to build but they can be of the simplest nature. One can often help a young child enter into the spirit of play, if they are having difficulty doing so, by inviting them to build a house that can quickly become a fort or any other structure, as they wish.

Make-believe Play: This is a broad category and when children engage in make-believe or imaginative play they usually incorporate many other types as well. They take on roles and typically begin a play session with the words, "Let's pretend I'm the Mommy and you're the Daddy," or "I'm a pirate and you're a sailor." The possibilities are endless as children play out roles they see around them in their family and community or roles they've heard of but not seen, such as witches or superheroes. Young children also love to play animal roles, both wild and domesticated. Make-believe play gives children an opportunity to try on every facet of life and make it their own. Children readily engage in make-believe play with their siblings and peers, but they also play on their own, quietly or in conversation with favorite dolls, stuffed animals, or imaginary friends.

Symbolic Play: Children will frequently take any object at hand and convert it into the toy they need. A stick becomes a fishing rod, a sword, a walking stick, or part of a house. A single object may become several things in one play scenario. A banana can serve as telephone one moment and be eaten the next. Children's minds are very fertile and providing them with open-ended materials rather than defined toys lets them exercise this type of play. For example one little girl had a favorite "rock baby" that she wrapped in flannel and cared for most lovingly, yet it was only a smooth river stone. It is also fascinating to introduce a new object into a play arena and see the many ways the children use it.

Language Play: Children use language in combination with other play types, especially in make-believe play, but they also play with language. They change words of verses and songs or make up their own. They tell stories and use voice, facial expression and gesture to enliven their language. Foreign languages fascinate them, especially when offered playfully in verse and song, which they readily learn.

Playing with the Arts: Children spontaneously integrate all forms of artistic activity into their play, using whatever materials are at hand to draw, model, or create music. They love puppets and will create puppet shows, especially after seeing one performed.

Sensory Play: Most children enjoy playing with sand, mud, water, and a host of objects with different textures, sounds, and smells.

Rough-and-Tumble Play: This is a very fundamental form of play that one sees in animals as well as in children. On the Internet there was a wonderful film of a polar bear and a husky dog spontaneously engaging in such play, narrated by Dr. Stuart Brown of the National Play Institute.[*] He points out the body language that differentiates such play from aggressive play. In rough and tumble play one typically sees rounded body gestures and a general spirit of playfulness rather than pointed aggression and a wish for dominance.

Risk-taking Play: Children like to flirt with danger and play on railroad tracks, climb trees, or do tricks on swings. Generally they have a good sense of how far to go without serious injury, especially if they've been given freedom to play with movement from a young age. Regrettably children are given very little opportunity for risk-taking today. Most play areas are designed to be as risk-free as possible, rather than providing as much risk as is reasonable. The lack of risk in childhood may account for some of the more extreme sports adolescents prefer.

Children with disabilities need to exercise as wide a range of play types as do other children, though they may be especially challenged in executing certain types of play. This is where the skills of recreation workers can be of great help.

One can add more and more categories as one watches children at play, for play is an incredibly varied and rich field of activity. It is ever changing and very individualized.. In addition to play types there are also differences in play by gender and by age. In open-ended play or child-organized sports it easy to integrate children of different ages, genders and abilities for the play is very flexible and the ever-changing rules accommodate the needs of all the children.

Why Play is So Important?

Play is a universal human activity of children around the world. While there are always individual differences in play

---

[*] Cf. http://www.nifplay.org/ (accessed July 4, 2017).

behaviors, there are also remarkable similarities in children's play. The variables are the societal norms the form the context of play. Most cultures recognize the importance of unstructured, child-led play and give children time to play alongside the time needed for school and for chores. In very poor areas children may be engaged in child labor that clearly curtails their playtime, but even then children are likely to use every little opportunity for play.

It is ironic that it is not just the poorest children who may lack time to play. In today's world, children of the middle class and wealthiest are also denied playtime in favor of a surfeit of adult-organized enrichment activities. These may be tutoring programs, sports programs or simply a combination of too many different activities outside school. Play is also eroded in North America by growing amounts of homework and long hours in front of screens. We often hear that the average American child sits in front of televisions, computers, and video screens for up to five hours per day outside school. This does not leave much time for active play.

Children do spend a growing amount of time with video games and some adults see this as a legitimate form of play. But the games are so heavily loaded with a story line created by adults that the input of the children seems minor in comparison. Likewise, most toys today come with a strong story line developed in television shows or movies. Children have little opportunity to develop their own play stories with the objects. This is especially true of battery-operated and high-tech toys, which tend to do the playing for the child.

If play is of such central importance to children's overall development, what happens when children are play-deprived? Scholars have only begun to study this, but early indications connect play deprivation with heightened aggression, as well as possible depression, hyperactive behaviors and even autism. In an article on play deprivation by playworker Bob Hughes of England, Play Wales, a national play advocacy organization, records distressing data about Romanian orphans who suffered extensive sensory and play deprivation. They suffered "severe learning difficulties, erratic behavior, and difficulty in forming bonds." Such findings are similar to those of animals that are play deprived. They become highly aggressive and show bizarre behaviors. They appear to lose touch with the social norms of their species.*

A growing recognition of the need for play and concern for its disappearance led the American Academy of Pediatrics to issue a far-reaching report in October 2006, calling upon pediatricians to discuss play with parents and help restore it to children's lives.

The report says, "Free and unstructured play is healthy and, in fact, essential for helping children reach important social, emotional, and cognitive developmental milestones as well as helping them manage stress and become resilient.... Whereas play protects children's emotional development, a loss of free time in combination with a hurried lifestyle can be a source of stress, anxiety and may even contribute to depression for many children."**

Gradually the American public is recognizing the importance of play and the serious consequences of its loss. As time is again allotted for play it is especially important that children of all abilities benefit. Many children with disabilities have been left on the sidelines of play in the past and it is critical that they be given full opportunities to play with their peers. Their need for play to support their overall development is as fundamental as for all other children and their capacity for play is as great.

---

*   Cf. http://www.playwales.org.uk/eng/ (accessed July 4, 2017).
**   Cf. http://www.aap.org/pressroom/play-public.htm (accessed July 4, 2017).

10

WILL

Schools do everything they can to promote and assess intelligence. In so many ways, the acquisition of knowledge is considered the main goal of educators. Lesson plans, tests, activities, and assignments are almost always designed to enhance intellectual learning. One could say that "head" knowledge and critical thinking are front and center in most classrooms. And most parents and teachers today could well say, *why not?*

Over the past couple of decades, the notion of emotional intelligence has gained currency, with greater emphasis on the maturation of our students and possibilities for them to learn to process their feelings. These involve such vital life skills as self-awareness, self-regulation, motivation, empathy, and relationship skills. When schools value and work with these aspects, children can learn to deal with "blind spots" and the particular lenses that they may use to filter experiences from home life to community norms, and they can learn how their own particular biases both filter and impact how we work together.

In his book, *Social Intelligence: The New Science of Success*, Karl Albrecht describes how emotional intelligence is related directly to social intelligence and five distinct areas of competence:

1. **Situational awareness.** We can think of this dimension as a kind of "social radar," or the ability to read situations and to interpret the behaviors of people in those situations

in terms of their possible intentions, emotional states, and proclivity to interact.

2. **Presence.** Often referred to as "bearing," presence incorporates a range of verbal and nonverbal patterns, one's appearance, posture, voice quality, subtle movements—a whole collection of signals others process into an evaluative impression of a person.

3. **Authenticity.** The social radars of other people pick up various signals from our behavior that lead them to judge us as honest, open, ethical, trustworthy, and well-intentioned—or inauthentic.

4. **Clarity.** Our ability to explain ourselves, illuminate ideas, pass data clearly and accurately, and articulate our views and proposed courses of action, enables us to get others to cooperate with us.

5. **Empathy.** Going somewhat beyond the conventional connotations of empathy as having a feeling for someone else, or "sympathizing" with them, we define empathy as a shared feeling between two people. In this connotation we will consider empathy a state of connectedness with another person, which creates the basis for positive interaction and cooperation. (Albrecht pp. 29–30)

Taking the first letter of each of the above, Albrecht then uses "S.P.A.C.E." as his shorthand as he explores these aspects of social intelligence. Indeed, so much of getting along with others has to do with boundaries and personal space.

The implications of these five points should be quite clear to readers of this book on nonviolence, because so much depends on the degree to which we all can work with self-education in life, and the degree to which we succeed or fail in our efforts. Generalizations are always dangerous, but my impression is that when acts of violence occur, there are usually antecedents and significant deficits among several if not all of the above five intelligences.

To the degree that teachers and parents are aware of the importance of both emotional and social intelligence, we have a real chance of making progress. And a curriculum, such as what is practiced in Waldorf schools, that gives the above competencies real time and space to develop, has a significant advantage over those that focus only on intellectual acuity.

These days many people value what can be called thinking (at least in the form of intelligence) and feeling (as discussed in relation to emotional and social intelligence). But one can hardly ever find any other educational system that so thoroughly also values and educates the will as does Waldorf. In our Waldorf schools, teachers consciously and concertedly work with both repetition and rhythm because they see them as huge catalysts for learning. For example, the morning circle in which the children sing, recite, and move together in practicing skills over time, is a prime example of repetition. By doing something again and again, even if somewhat unconsciously, the children gain strength and certainty in their lessons. Practicing a musical instrument or a sport has the same effect.

Genius is more learned than a given, as indicated in Malcolm Gladwell's 10,000-hour rule. Examples of Bill Gates in his high school computer lab, or Mozart playing piano as a very young child are often cited as contributing to acquired "genius," not to mention star Canadian hockey players who were born early in the calendar year, thus providing an edge on their southern neighbors! It is what Gladwell in his book *Outliers* calls the "accumulative advantage," which results later in superior results. Doing something again and again, whether 10,000 hours or not, allows for the possibility of mastery—not a guarantee, but a huge advantage. Repetition requires disciplined will. Human potential is unlimited.

Another aspect is rhythm. Returning to a subject, as Waldorf teachers do in three- or four-week main lesson blocks, or concentrated study for two hours every morning, further develops competencies. When I taught Botany in fifth grade in the autumn, there were distinct seasonal advantages to outdoor education. So it was again when I returned to the subject in a three week concentrated block in the spring of that year. Yet what often goes unspoken in pedagogical discussion was the interval *in between the two blocks*—likewise, history, physics, and many others subjects. As with seasonality, rhythm brings maturation and depth. Even in the daily rhythm of opening and closing a main lesson, the children learn to breathe into the day; they are able to relate on levels beyond cognitive functioning. They *live into* the experiences when they return to them in rhythmic succession. Repetition and rhythm are fundamentally educational.

The will that manifests as activity connects us to the natural world and its lawfulness. When we garden, stack wood, or rake leaves we are connecting with primordial nature forces. New Hampshire oak and maple leaves speak back to us in a way that cordwood does not. We can try and *think* our way through a lawn covered with leaves, or *feel* a relationship to stacking wood (and there is nothing wrong with these wishes), but in the end, one has to move limbs and actually do the work to get the job done, and that takes *will*.

But the issue is far deeper than leaves and cordwood. We know from Rudolf Steiner that the will is also mysteriously connected to human destiny (*Anthroposophical Leading Thoughts*, pp. 30–31). The facts of nature speak only to a portion of human reality. Raking leaves or stacking wood is observable but does not explain fully who is doing the work. There is a larger dimension to all that has been willed into existence in my person—what I call "myself" in this lifetime. One could say that what I have become in this life is due in no small part to the working of destiny.

Then there is an enigmatic statement in the previously cited text by Rudolf Steiner, a suggestion that puzzles me to no end. After speaking of the spiritual nature of the will comes this phrase: "Then the Good and the Evil will be severally realized" (ibid., p. 31). This hints at a moral force in the will. We are, in a sense, fashioned not just by heredity and our environment, but also by the willing arising from our previous earthly life. An "image" so to speak, was formed of our intentions, and we willed those intentions into physical reality with our birth on Earth.

This is indeed food for thought. It places the issues of risk factors, the friends we meet, and the challenges we face in a whole new light. It does not explain away or by any means condone behavior, but it helps us understand our human encounters beyond the usual environmental influences. Yes, poverty matters. If a person is born into a home in which a parent is an addict, this matters. But the preceding thoughts add another dimension. For the teacher or parent who struggles to work with a challenging child, the very challenges themselves may be a call from a far distant place and time. Our most challenging students are often those who have the most to teach us. They are the ones we need to welcome with extra open-heartedness, for in them we often hear destiny speaking most clearly.

11

Peace through Wholeness

In most schools today, the main focus is on developing intelligence. We need clear thinking, intelligent human beings to help us solve problems and innovate. But when the emphasis is almost exclusively on the intellect at the expense of other human attributes, we run the risk of one-sided, abstract learning that separates people from one another and from real situations in the world around us. Focusing too much on the intellect results in clever human beings who can criticize better than they can engage. Abstraction and disconnection can lead to antisocial behavior and do real harm to relationships.

In his novel, *Collision*, my father describes two executives in a corporate setting: one who primarily uses his intellect and one who operates more from the heart. With the excitement of a suspense novel, these two individuals eventually clash, and the heart person suffers tremendously in the short term. There is something truly cruel about anyone who uses pure intellect for the ruthless achievement of wealth and power. It is not until the second book, *Lonely Expiation*, that the more balanced one (Lucinda) finds a way forward again—in part by discovering biodynamic farming and Waldorf education.

Indeed, Waldorf education is known for its emphasis on "wholeness" by fostering the healthy development of the "head, heart, and hands" of each child. One of the primary vehicles for this is the use of artistic methods of education to awaken capacities in children. Rather than simply pouring in new concepts, Waldorf educators seek first to awaken themselves through self-development and professional growth, and then they awaken children through sensory-rich, imaginative teaching. Storytelling, creation of main lesson books, painting, circle games, and singing all contribute to an environment of beauty and meaning.

Most of all, teachers begin from "the whole" and then go to the parts. In first grade, I taught numbers by describing the number one as the whole world, the unity of the universe, the completeness of being one class. Only then did we go to the number two, day and night, and the other aspects of three, four, etc. This continued later on in algebra, when we began with the whole equation and then learned the specific skills and properties. In history, we used biography to describe a particular person in the context of his or her times and geographic place on the Earth. Everything in Waldorf is a "whole" before it becomes the parts.

This is in contrast to many practices elsewhere in which things are taught in a logical, incremental series of "units" that end up, we hope, with a sense for the sum total experience. These isolated concepts often wither on the vine, and we see from years and years of teaching to the test that the results are less than hoped for. SAT scores have not really gone anywhere despite massive investment of technology and new curriculum. (By the way, I am all in favor of technology at an age-appropriate level and used as a tool and not an end in itself.) Nevertheless, abstract learning, devoid of real content and experience, isolates human beings from themselves and each other. As will be described in other sections of this book, isolation and disconnection are two of the building blocks of deviant behavior and possible acts of violence.

Teaching which is living, experiential, age appropriate, and artistic can place a child in the world who sees how all things are related, makes connections between ideas, and sees the totality of human relationships in the context of community. This leads to real capacities such as imagination, problem solving, critical thinking, social sensitivity, and more that can withstand the test of time and a variety of job contexts in a future career.

In his lectures to teachers, Rudolf Steiner often spoke of the need for students to be engaged both in contemplation and activity so that they experience a kind of tension and relaxation—an alternation between passive absorption of stories, history, and didactic teaching and hands-on engagement in projects:

> Essentially our lessons consist of two interacting parts. We instruct, we exhort the children to participate, to use their skills, to be physically active. Be it eurythmy, music, physical education, even writing or the mechanical process in arithmetic—we try to engender activity. The other part of our lesson is concerned with contemplation. Here we ask the children to think about, to consider the things we tell them. (Steiner, *Education for Adolescents,* p. 20)

He goes on to say that too much contemplation (which I would maintain is the norm in many schools) makes the student "benumbed" and leads them to become confused adults. Too much contemplation enhances a kind of sleep-like activity. But when we balance contemplation with activity such as projects, music, and movement, we wake them up and enhance engagement with the world. A good teacher takes any subject that might appear dry or abstract and makes it come alive by relating it to the human being, showing how all things are related to the student. "By relating the outer world to the human being we always stimulate their feelings—and this is so very important" (ibid., p. 24). For example, in teaching thermodynamics or any science, a teacher might make a side comment connected to fever or some aspect of the home.

How does all of this relate to a nonviolent education? These themes are covered again in other contexts in this book, but in regard to the above passages, one can say: education that puts a one-sided emphasis on intellectual contemplation (and then continually "testing" for the "facts" without proper digestion of the material) is a violation of human nature. Children subjected to this kind of educational abuse, when accompanied by any latent family, environmental, or soul predispositions, are more likely to take extreme measures to rebalance. When children have not had balance in teaching, especially a healthy engagement with meaningful activity, they can strike out as an act of desperation.

The soul seeks balance, and when not provided in the course of a school day, it can take radical alternatives. Some children will seek balance on their own in after school activities, or in the case of young children, in play. Some get very involved in sports, drama, or music after school, thus rebalancing some of what was neglected during the school day. But in some cases, those activities are not available or are insufficient, leading to antisocial actions. It is vitally important for teachers and parents to realize that a balance of theory and practice during the school day is essential to healthy human development.

Another way of making this point is to say that what goes "in" through contemplation and listening needs to find "external" expression through projects, arts, and movement. Rather than suppressing what has been heard, the student needs to bring the concepts into expression and relate them to the outer world. Eurythmy, for example, makes visible what goes on inwardly in listening, and in doing so, the child's self finds new ways to relate to the world. What is inner can become outer; listening becomes meaningful movement, which in turn enhances the listening:

> Our listening, especially with verbs, is in reality always a form of participation. What is at this time the most spiritual part of the human being participates; it simply suppresses the activity.
> Only in eurythmy is this activity placed in the external world. In addition to all its other benefits, eurythmy also activates listening. When one person says something, the other listens; one engages in the "I" with what lives physically in the sounds, but suppresses it. The "I" always participates in eurythmy, and what eurythmy puts before us through the physical body is nothing other than listening made visible. You always do eurythmy when you listen, and when you actually perform eurythmy you are just making visible what remains invisible when you listen. The manifestation of the activity of the listening human being is, in fact, eurythmy. It is not something arbitrary, but rather the revelation of the activity of the listening human being. (Steiner, *Practical Advice to Teachers,* pp. 56–57)

In eurythmy the children are given not only hygiene of the body, as in gymnastics, but also hygiene of the soul (Richards, p. 66).

There is one more benefit beyond "hygiene of the soul," and that is enhanced memory. When teachers work as described here by Rudolf Steiner, and when the students' feelings are stirred by active participation, they remember better! They identify with the material; the content of the "lessons" becomes part of a treasure trove of personal possessions, and like anything memorable, it becomes easier to recall. Thus, by teaching less to the test and by engaging more in real activity, students actually remember more and do better on tests when they are relevant.

It is a sad commentary on many classrooms today that what is taking place in the name of improving nationwide test scores is actually undermining real achievement. Standardized testing and a curriculum designed to focus mostly on memorization and rote learning actually has the opposite of its intended results. Waldorf teachers, and all who are progressive educators, are building a true foundation for learning and improving academic results by using balance in teaching.

Of course, there are also social implications. When given the opportunity for experiential learning, children start to notice the world around them again. With just a little direction, they can connect with other people in meaningful ways. For example, my children's Waldorf teachers have often given them assignments in which they have to "interview" someone in the community. Ionas was recently assigned to speak with someone who had emigrated from another country. Though there were a few days of bemoaning "another assignment," when he actually did the interview, he was enthused! His class recently took a field trip to a prison, and Ionas had a chance to ask questions of the inmates. (Ionas asked, "What is the best and worst part of your day?") These experiences lead to sharing over the dinner table at home—yet another aspect of healthy social development.

Thus, part of an education for nonviolence involves noticing the world around us and taking interest in other people, especially those who are not like us. Rather than shutting the door to our country or our hearts by seeing only individuals who might appear to be like us, we need to open the doors and windows. This can lead to new respect for those who have traveled different pathways, and along the way, we learn to listen with new sensitivity. Rudolf Steiner connects this with teaching grammar in the elementary grades:

> Now that you know that when you speak a noun you dissociate yourself from your environment, that when you speak an adjective you unite yourself with your surroundings, and that when you speak a verb you blossom out into

your environment and move with it, you will speak with a very different inner emphasis about the noun, the adjective, and the verb than you would if you were unaware of these facts. (Steiner, *Practical Advice*, p. 58)

Even simple routines in a Waldorf classroom serve to establish the habits of care, consideration, and community: cleaning the classroom, recycling and taking out the compost, helping a peer who is struggling with an assignment, the personal morning handshake, check in with the class teacher at the door, cleaning paintbrushes and boards after using them.... The list goes on and on. These tasks are not just about getting the job done. Far more important are the life skills and the social consciousness that develops when a group of children can participate in a continuous learning environment over many years. The children are learning the social art of cohabitation on this Earth, and in so doing develop deep roots of resiliency. M. C. Richards has strong words for those schools that ignore these social principles:

> The world of forming, as experienced from the inside, as process coming into being, is not the world of most of the public schools. Knowledge is packaged in plastic covers or stored in electronic circuits. To many children it seems dehumanized and abstract. Students tend to be overwhelmed by the apparatus and complexity before they have really experienced themselves as source.
> The experiencing of oneself as source, human being as source, the history humankind as a source, evolution of consciousness as source, future unfolding as source—this is a formative factor in the Waldorf schooling. And it accounts, for example, for such principles as teaching of writing before reading, and the fact that the curriculum follows the history of human consciousness....
> The form of the class is an expression of social and moral attitudes. Faithfulness, flexibility, and diversity of abilities are affirmed. If there is trouble in the relationship between teacher and pupils, it will have to be worked out as in a family.

Students and teachers learn to get along, to give and take, to accept, to forgive, to change, to adapt, and to develop humor and warmth that don't quit. (Richards, pp. 70–71)

Finally, when education is seen as an art and not just a science, it is possible to awaken capacities in the children that further build resiliency and social maturity. Rather than bottling things up until they explode in violent emotion or physical acts, children need to be given constructive outlets for their energy. Modeling with clay, carving wood, knitting socks, learning to draw, and writing poetry all provide different modalities and opportunities for self-expression. Through a living experience of working with a medium that responds, that shows the intent of the creator, and that does not lie in both success and failure, artistic practice educates emotional intelligence and accountability. In throwing a bowl in a workshop, one can mess up again and again, but it does no good to blame the clay or the wheel. It is you yourself, the person who is responsible for all the outcomes, and that leads to self-education and control of both hands and the intentions that flow through them. In mastering an art form, we learn to master ourselves.

12

UNCONDITIONAL HOSPITALITY

Jesus said, "I was a stranger and you welcomed me."

In a wonderful book titled *Making Room*, Christine Pohl begins with a description of the historical context of hospitality and the age-old social desire to welcome strangers, give mutual aid, and demonstrate neighborliness as an expression of faith. In Romans 15:7, Paul urges believers to "receive one another as Christ received us." Even today we know the joy of being welcomed and the pain when one is excluded.

From the early stages of simply opening the home to travelers, the practice evolved to include hostels, hospices, and for those who were ailing, hospitals. Providing for others was an expression of social responsibility. In the Middle Ages, the practice at times deviated from care of the needy to become an expression of largess, of power and influence in a community. One opened one's home for visiting dignitaries, provided food and entertainment, often with the aim of cementing alliances. By the eighteenth century, hospitality had become an antiquated practice that was out of step with commercial practices such as the renting of a room for the night. Urbanization and industrialization came with increased concern about privacy and the risks involved in offering hospitality to strangers. Both guests and hosts seemed to feel a greater sense of vulnerability when hospitality was hidden from view, which increased the role of institutions and a lessening of faith based hospitality:

> The long-term consequences of identifying hospitality with civic and domestic spheres were significant. The public and civic dimensions of hospitality—from hospitals, poor relief, and responsibility to refugees, to later concerns about human rights and equality—became detached from the Christian roots as the public sphere was increasingly secularized. At the same time, the domestic sphere became more privatized; households became smaller, more intimate, and less able or willing to receive strangers. (Pohl, p. 53)

Yet, even in more recent times, hosts seem to face a challenge:

> The story of the Village Le Chambon is a powerful example of the meaning of difference in practice of hospitality. This small community of French Protestants rescued Jews during World War II. Opening homes, schools, and churches to strangers with quiet, steady hospitality, they made Le Chambon the safest place in Europe for Jews. When the police asked the pastor of the community to turn in Jews, Andre Trocme responded, "we do not know what a Jew is. We know only of men." His response is profoundly illuminating. When, by acknowledging differences, we only endanger, then we must only acknowledge a common human identity. (ibid., p. 83)

Hospitality, both past and present, has at its core the ideal of social justice. In recent times Europe has experienced a flood of refugees from Syria and other countries fleeing war and persecution. This has forced hosting countries to confront questions of diversity, religion, and inclusion. Long held social ideals such as open borders have come up against physical challenges of simply accommodating so many new people. Communities have had to grapple with issues of identity and integration. In the multicultural society of today many feel fragmented and disconnected as never before. Some feel the loss of the bonds that used to give meaning to life, yet others want to demonstrate compassion and concern for those less fortunate. Both those who have been displaced, refugees and the homeless, and those attempting to welcome strangers feel an alienation from the past and estrangement from old customs. Everything appears to be in flux.

It is a sign of our time that issues of homelessness and the plight of refugees have confronted affluence and material comfort in so many countries today. Where do we stand in regard to social justice today? Often those who have the least provide the most. The Middle Eastern church at Antioch, though not wealthy, cared for 3,000 widows and virgins daily, as well as those in prison, the sick, and the disabled who were far from home. Some came daily for food and clothing, as is true of community centers across North America today.

> Offers of food or a meal together are central to almost all biblical stories of hospitality, to most historical discussions of hospitality, and to almost every contemporary practice of hospitality. In the context of shared meals, Jesus frequently challenged the prevailing religious and cultural boundaries by the company he kept and exposed hidden patterns of social exclusion. He was a guest in the home of tax collectors, dined with sinners, and taught hosts to welcome those most likely to be excluded....
>
> Practitioners recognize the relationship between justice and shared meals. Ed Loring, of the Open Door Community in Atlanta, observed that "justice is important, but supper is essential." His comment in no way reduces the importance of sustained efforts at social justice, to which the entire community is committed. But, Murphy Davis, cofounder of the Open Door, explained, "Without supper, without love, without table companionship, justice can become a program that we *do* to other people" (ibid., pp. 73–74)

Breaking bread together has long been a centerpiece of hospitality. This practice has deep roots in biblical traditions, from the feeding of five thousand to the Last Supper (see more on this in another chapter). The living bread and water offer more than physical sustenance. The shared meal, often still today accompanied by good conversation, binds people together in fellowship. In many faith-based homes, sharing food connects people to their spiritual origins and reminds them that it is not by bread alone that we live.

> The Eucharist most fundamentally connects hospitality with God because it anticipates and reveals the "heavenly table of the Lord." In that sacrament, we are nourished on our journey toward God's banquet table, even as we experience the present joy and welcome associated with sharing in that table. A shared meal is the activity most closely tied to the reality of God's Kingdom, just as it is the most basic expression of hospitality....
>
> The theological importance of eating together helps explain why practitioners of hospitality so often report that they feel closest to God in times of shared meals.... A practitioner explains, "Everyone wants to be at supper because if you miss that, you missed everything. It is here that we recognize Jesus in the breaking of the bread." A woman, recalling her childhood experience of revivals in the black church tradition, remembers the mealtimes as the most powerful and holy part of the week. In many communities of hospitality, meals, and worship are regularly intertwined....
>
> One of the key Greek words for hospitality, *philoxenia,* combines the general word for love or affection for people who are connected by kinship or faith (*phileo*), and the word for stranger (*xenos*). Thus, etymologically and practically, in the New Testament, hospitality is closely connected to love. Because *philoxenia* includes the word for stranger, hospitality's orientation toward strangers is also more apparent in Greek than in English. (ibid., pp. 30–31)

Thus in many traditions hospitality was a sign of leadership in a community. Those who volunteer, help with the distribution of food and clothing, are not only performing good deeds but also exercising civic responsibility and servant leadership.

Unconditional Hospitality

Today more than ever we need to recognize the eternal in every human being. Some of the most remarkable people on this Earth can come in "the stranger's guise." Often the initial encounter is uneventful, even commonplace. Yet once in a while one ends up having a short conversation in which a phrase or a few key words live on for days afterward. What often occurs to me in such random encounters is that *in the particular is revealed the eternal, in the sentence fragment live words of truth.* The cynic might say that this is due to how we interpret, the context we ourselves bring to the moment. But I have learned that one can often learn the most from unexpected sources such as young children, the infirm, and the homeless. In these cases something *speaks through the person* and we are all the better for the human encounter.

In a book that is mostly autobiographical, my father chose the title *Footprints of an Angel*, in which he tells stories of his life from the vantage point of a higher perspective. Looking back on things that happened in his life, from selling bibles to looking for a job, he illustrates how many life-changing events cannot be understood by everyday logic. In fact, particularly in human encounters, one can sense the presence of one's personal angel, another intelligent presence.

We need to remember that even strangers have angels, and when we open our doors and our hearts, we have a chance to meet them. Shared meals, community potlucks, Thanksgiving dinner, and the holiday faire are more than opportunities to socialize or raise money. They are invitations for hosting the higher presence of "the other." One could thus say that hospitality is both horizontal, sharing food around a table, and vertical, invoking a presence that could not be there without us. *"We always treat guests as angels—just in case"* (Brother Jeremiah of Wallachia).

While attending a meeting at the Goetheanum in Dornach, Switzerland, some time ago, we were asked to select a person we did not know and go for a walk. The assignment was to discuss the place or country where we feel most at home. So for thirty or forty minutes, we all wandered up and down the footpaths of that particular hill. Afterward we came back as a large group and shared a few experiences. One of the most remarkable for me was the observation that many reported a sense of homelessness, not being rooted in one place or country. Of course most had homes and jobs, but, inwardly, there was a common feeling of being free of old constraints and geographical roots. I came away with the message that, in a sense, many human beings today are people without a place, strangers in their own land.

To be a stranger means to be somewhat detached, even while still performing duties at work and at home. Even those with financial resources can feel unattached to any one particular place or location. This is of course not exactly the same as those who live homeless on the street, but on a spiritual level I feel we are all refugees, fleeing, but not always knowing our eventual destination.

Pohl shares a few more vignettes from the story of hospitality:

> Several Old Testament accounts show hospitality beginning in a public place where the community gathered regularly. The stranger was first encountered there and then invited into an individual household. Hospitality begins at the gate, in the doorway, on bridges between public and private space. Finding and creating threshold places is important for the contemporary expressions of hospitality....
>
> Pilgrims were among the first masses of people who were detached from place and societal relationships; few had significant connections with hosts along the way. Many more beggars, combining the vulnerabilities of the poor and the stranger; some pilgrims were criminals and adventures.... Poor pilgrims, especially, where handled at

a distance, at the gate or in institutions set up for them; rarely were they welcomed into the center of the household. (ibid., pp. 95–98)

Today there are those who are hidden in prisons and facilities for extended care. To help them, one has to enter their world and feel oneself a stranger in an unfamiliar place. Those today who work with hospice enter homes as strangers but end up forging real bonds of friendship with both the dying and the surrounding family.

Then there are the stories of remarkable women who served the poor in extraordinary ways:

> From historical records we know that women such as Melania, Marcella, Paula and Eustochium offered generous hospitality to the poor, often exhausting their family resources. Jerome provides a long testimony to Fabiola's charity and hospitality. She was a Roman matron (d. 399) with enormous wealth who had spent time in Bethlehem with Jerome, Paula and Eustochium. Fabiola later returned to Rome, where she continued vast charitable works. Jerome described her return: she, "who only had traveling baggage and was a stranger in every land, returned to her native city to live in poverty where she had been rich, to lodge in the house of another, she who had once entertained many guests." Jerome praised her generosity, humility, simple dress, and intensity of faith....
>
> For these women, the practice of hospitality combined servanthood with influence. Hospitality entailed the deepest acts of humility and service when offered to the poor, sick, or strangers....
>
> Dorothy Day in her book *House of Hospitality*, wrote that "The ideal, of course, would be that each Christian...should take in one of the homeless as an honored guest, remembering Christ words: 'inasmuch as ye have done it unto the least of these, ye have done it unto me.'" She noted that in her experience "the poor are more conscious of this obligation than those who are comfortably off." (ibid., pp. 107–116)

Yet there is also a cautionary note:

> Without a healthy acknowledgment of their own frailties and needs, the host can take on very patronizing attitudes. But hosts must also be able to move through their own brokenness to welcome others....
>
> There is a complex dance between recognizing our own need, ministering to those in need, and recognizing their ministry to us. The helper must also be able to receive—especially from those who look as if they have little to offer....
>
> In other communities there is a significant reconfiguration of roles when guests do some or all of the cooking. Shared tasks break down barriers and have the potential for equalizing some relations. There is a sense of camaraderie that emerges and spills over as all sit down to eat together. There are situations in which everyone is a stranger and some of the strangers must take on the role of the hosting to establish any community or relationship. In groups of displaced persons such as refugees or migrants, no one feels "home." (ibid., pp. 118–123)

"If there is room in the heart, there is room in the house."
—Danish proverb

The themes sounded in these passages support the case for education toward peace, albeit in this case, peace in the home and community. Children spend a significant amount of time in school, but home and community are also extremely influential. We can put it in a series of questions:

1. Does the family "break bread" together at least once a day? When that happens, conversation can occur, family ties are nourished, and there is a sense of "home" even if family members are scattered at work and school for the rest of the day.
2. Are guests welcome? Most times friends and family members visit, but that is a limited form of hospitality, and Pohl would argue that just having relatives and close friends can

become another form of self-aggrandizement. It is not the same as welcoming someone who is not an extension of a set circle of influence.
3. When guests are welcome, how are they received? There is a wide spectrum from being patronizing to being truly selfless.
4. Are we able to occasionally step outside our personal shelter and visit with those who are bereft of such luxury? Volunteering in a community kitchen, shelter for abused women, a prison, or halfway house is a very different form of hospitality.
5. Are we honest with ourselves in facing our continuing struggle to see the eternal (the angel) in another person? I find this easy in the abstract, but challenging when faced with a real life situation, especially when there is conflict.
6. What have I done recently on behalf of social justice? It may be easy to write about, talk about, discuss over dinner, but what have I actually done? Some may think one has to travel to a distant country to work with those who are struggling, but what about closer to home? Issues of equity, language, and attitudes play out in even the most everyday workplace situations.

These are but a half-dozen questions arising from the above chapter, yet I would maintain that the answers, when honestly arrived at, go a long way toward building a more peaceful world. Our children notice how we speak to each other, how we relate at the dinner table, who is welcome and who is not, and these observations are formative. Experiences in the home and in community can support or hinder sound decisions in teenage years and beyond. And the social fabric is woven by the many, many small decisions each one of us makes on a daily basis.

13

Forgiveness and the Last Supper

As I lived with the topics covered in the foregoing chapters of this book, I have found again and again that some of the social challenges in the world around us today often stem from small injustices that fester and grow over time. One such instance has to do with betrayal. Often unspoken or left unresolved, a small "hurt" can grow into interpersonal friction, tension between groups, or even a larger "cause." Often we externalize what could have been dealt with in the early stages.

I asked some of my friends and students for examples of their experiences with instances of an everyday sense of betrayal, and these are some of the things that I heard:

1. Something said to a friend or colleague in confidence, only to find out later that it was passed on to others;
2. A moment in a meeting when you needed a word of encouragement or recognition and nothing happened;
3. The so called "silent treatment." They have experienced betrayal not just in what was spoken but in the absence of words that should have been spoken in a given moment in time;
4. When you looked up to someone, respected someone for years, and suddenly you saw that person doing something wrong, telling a small lie, doing something that is borderline unethical;

5. Overt lies that can elicit a sense of betrayal, but much more difficult at times are...;
6. Slight evasions of the truth, a sidestepping that can appear harmless at first and then seem more troubling with time.

This then calls us to ask: What do we do when we encounter these larger or smaller instances of betrayal? Do we accept these stated instances simply as part of life—as just aspects of living in today's world? However, when any of these occurrences become a pattern, when someone you know repeatedly evades the truth or repeatedly fails to recognize you and so on, then something starts to set in at a deeper level. Some of the sources I consulted spoke about how minor instances of betrayal can easily escalate over time into major, intentional acts of betrayal. This happens, in part, as people take these instances to heart, dwell on them, and then form picture memories that can evolve over time. What started out as a few poorly chosen words can, over time, morph into a whole complex of verbal interactions that become self-reinforcing.

I had a student in my office recently in tears due to an act of betrayal from a friend that occurred years ago. She still suffered from a sense of loss, a sense of frustration, and anger as a result of that particular experience.

One of the things that I have been working with is the question of how often money can play into these moments of betrayal. For some reason, there is a quality to the financial transaction that often leaves people a bit on edge. I often find with Waldorf teachers, for example, that they will have the most amazing conversation about the children in faculty meetings—they will do a child study, they will prepare a festival, they will talk about the third-grade curriculum—and one senses that these are all people who have found their higher selves and that they are working out of their higher selves. Then later in the agenda, there is a topic called "the budget," the scholarship program, or something similar, and suddenly the whole conversation goes downhill. It is very interesting to see how this happens. Some of the more poignant examples of betrayal that I have heard about and personally experienced often involve matters of money.

Thanks to Brien Masters and a wonderful little book he wrote on the Oberufer Christmas plays, I was reminded of Mary and Joseph looking for a place to stay and the words of the second innkeeper: "Bah, what's this? Beggars on my life. / What care I, fellow, for you and your wife? / I take in folks with money in purse..." There is that thing of money. Mary and Joseph and, of course, the innkeepers (especially the second) had no idea of what was really presenting itself to them in the doorway. But then fast forward thirty-three years and we have the infamous thirty pieces of silver paid to Judas. It is very interesting that this whole story, the birth to thirty-three years later, is weighed in this equation of money and the uses of money. There is something there that really speaks of betrayal.

My brother Mark Finser has spent years working in social finance and studying Anthroposophy. I asked him to comment on this topic of betrayal, particularly in relation to money. This is what he said:

> My experience is that the human condition today is to pretty early on in our lives have a "money biography." Often, when we look back in our lives, we will see that it's in years ten, eleven, or twelve that our experiences with money set the tone for our whole lives on how we get affected by issues around money.... You could say the ultimate betrayal for humanity is the denial of reincarnation.
>
> The other theme that I have spent some time with is Steiner's *Fifth Gospel*, in which he talks about the three temptations of Christ. Since the Christ being had only just

been incarnated very briefly, this great being was not able to fully answer the challenge of turning stones into bread. As a result, this theme around work and money will remain with us throughout this Earth evolution. In there, Steiner also speaks that if we don't take steps to separate labor/work from our pay, it will be hard for humanity to truly experience the laws of reincarnation. That's why at RSF [Rudolf Steiner Foundation] we pay prospectively so as, in a small way, to make the staff conscious that they are not being paid for their work but they are being compensated so that they CAN work. You should see their faces when on their first day of work (their new job) they get a paycheck handed to them.

The other piece I wanted to mention is very interesting references I have encountered in *The Temple Legend* (Steiner) about Cain and Abel. We know that story well. Even when I taught it as a third grade teacher, I basically just told the story, as we know it. But what I have been working with more recently is what lies beneath the surface. Cain, as you know, is the one who is tilling the soil, trying to do the job and get something done. There is a part of all of us that is in that mode: "I've got to get to work today, and I have fifteen things I have to do, and I need to accomplish things." It is conquering the soil and the Earth, very much the part of all of us that has more of a masculine gesture. And then Abel, the tender of the flocks of sheep, the herder, the one who is nurturing and caring, who is working with growth and development and, perhaps, is not so intent on turning a profit or making money.

And so, in the story of Cain and Abel we have the one aspect of human nature overcoming, or slaying, the other. In evolution in general, Cain represents that part of our consciousness which is more Earth-centered, what wants to get things done on this Earth.

However, what I tried to do, and I have only gotten so far with it, is to try to put myself in the shoes of Cain. I always thought more about Abel; my heart always went out to Abel. It is like our hearts going out to the people who were killed recently in Oregon. That is the first thing that happens, your heart goes out. To put yourself in the shoes of the perpetrator of a crime is more of a struggle, at least for me. In thinking of Cain, I have come to the idea that, in a sense, there is a kind of betrayal at work here of one's own brother. Cain offered a sacrifice, and it was rejected.

Living with that story, I came to the idea that there is often something living underneath a betrayal; it is not merely a wanton act. And in the case of Cain, I imagine the bitterness, the frustration, the resentment at not having your sacrifice accepted (which can be seen as a kind of spiritual betrayal).

I then looked at some of the acts of betrayal in everyday life: At first, betrayal may manifest as an something external, but may also be a consequence of things going on within the human soul: resentment, frustration, unresolved conflict or just disappointment. If a person is being "difficult" in a social situation, such as within a group of colleagues, I have often found that, when you sit down and have a conversation and really get to know the context, there is often something working in the soul life with which one has to reckon. There might be an unhappy person deep down.

Now let us take a look at the other side: forgiveness. I am just amazed at the possibilities presented at the Last Supper. How is it that anyone could forgive or could knowingly forgive before the deed actually happens? That quality of forgiving beforehand, that is a very tall order! I reached back to Sergei O. Prokofieff, one of my favorites, for his book *The Occult Significance of Forgiveness*. He speaks of *milde*, a quality of gentleness, of mildness. "On the way toward initiation, the medieval hero Parsifal had to develop *milde*." Wolfgang von Eschenbach, in his version of the story, also uses the word *zelde*, which is related to the gothic *sehle*, meaning goodness, gentleness and blessed. According to Sergei, "Developing these soul qualities within oneself means creating the conditions that allow the cosmic spirit to descend into our "I" as the spirit self, that is that spirit with whom the Christ prophetically endows his apostles when he sends them out into the world to forgive men in his name and remit their sins" (Prokofieff, p. 117).

In the next step in my research I came across a fragment of an article published many years ago and I had to write to the ASA library in Ann Arbor, where they had a complete collection of *Journal for Anthroposophy*. There I found an article by Georg Kühlewind on forgiveness; if you think Prokofieff is dense, try reading Kühlewind! Nonetheless, his insights are amazing. When he uses a word such as *cognize*, it is more than the way we ordinarily use the term. He is talking about something that is really a spiritual deed. This is what Kühlewind has to say about forgiveness as a kind of mirrored consciousness, a fascinating concept: "In the meditative consciousness, however, we must experience the becoming with, the transformation into what is cognized. There is no other way. It is self-surrender, self-extinguishing pain." He takes this pathway of self-extinguishing, letting go; a painful experience as part of forgiveness. Then in the very next sentence, he takes the opposite tact: "It is joy, the coming into being in the other, realization, accomplishment." Kühlewind then sums it all up by saying in words that we all can understand, "Today's misfortune can prove to be a blessing...the joy of today can prove to be a tragic error."

It is a very interesting twist there with the forgiveness. We are reminded of the Goethe piece about seeing people as they are becoming and not just focusing on how they are in the moment. Kühlewind is all about this transformation that can occur, whether it is that path of self-forgetting and self-annihilation and the pain, or it is the path of joy and affirmation and the discovery of the other person. Both are possible through forgiveness.

I don't know how it is for you, but when you have those few moments to share personal experiences with a friend, suddenly something comes back that you may have forgotten, and then you see something also in a new light. Recently what came back to me was something that happened many years ago when I was a teenager. My friends and I were leaving the school after a concert. We were laughing and talking loudly as we walked down the hall; my cello was in my arms. Then we had the misfortune to encounter a custodian who had been drinking. He started chasing us. There were about half a dozen of us leaving the school, and as he chased us down the hallways, all my friends scattered. I was left running down a side hallway alone, hoping to get out the door at the end, but I found the door was locked. I remember standing there and having this guy come at me, lunging with his fists. The pain was partly physical—I was hospitalized as a result—but the pain inside that my friends had all run off, that also really got to me. It is funny how these things are psychological as well as physical. There is always a sort of silver lining to it, because one of the girls in the high school that I had long admired, (though she had never seemed to notice me at all), came to sit by my side in the hospital. Much was left unspoken, as so often happens at that age.

Of course, I have long forgiven the custodian. It is interesting that this was at Krefeld Freie Waldofschule in Germany. It turns out that a strong pioneer teacher at the school had hired the custodian, and as a result he worked there for years even though everyone knew he would drink at night. As a result of the investigation that followed, it turned out that the two individuals had actually served together as Nazis and that there was a connection that went way back. They had hidden it so well that no one found out about it until this incident occurred. Thus, in a way, the school had to go through this painful moment to come out the other side and face something that they wanted to avoid. They all knew the custodian had problems; they did not know about the connections that went way back.

The Last Supper is perhaps the ultimate example of this dynamic of betrayal and forgiveness. What is really happening in the amazing scene of these people sitting around the table in Leonardo's masterpiece? The story portrayed by his *Last Supper* is more than a great work of art; it is more than recounting a biblical event. Something else is moving through it. This comes from Rudolf Steiner's lecture on Leonardo:

> We see these twelve disciples, with deeply expressive movements and bearings, we see the gestures and attitudes of each of the twelve figures, so individualized, that we may well receive the impression that every form of the human soul, and character, finds expression in them. Every way in which a soul would relate itself, according to its particular temperament and character to what the picture expresses, is embodied in them. Leonardo's *Last Supper* seems the first to conjure up before us, with full dramatic force, an expression of very significant psychic conditions. (Feb. 13, 1913)

The Last Supper is really a representation of humanity. It is a picture of the whole. We see the parts, we see the individuals, but together it is an expression of the whole. If we want to reach some understanding of collaborative leadership, servant leadership, working harmoniously, and working in groups, there might be lessons in this picture we can carry away and work with. That was my starting point. Then I went down some pathways, byways, and other avenues, and I will share a few of them and try to draw it all together.

The first is the whole aspect of twelve. We have the twelve hours in the day, twelve hours in the night. We have the twelve months of the year and the twelve disciples. And when we start to live with the twelve plus the one, we go back in time and find that there is a deep Rosicrucian theme in this. There is the moment in the Rosicrucian mysteries when the chosen one is surrounded by the twelve teachers who impart knowledge of the whole world and everything that exists in the cosmos to the one at the center. According to *The Chymical Wedding of Christian Rosenkreutz*, this is a deeply Rosicrucian aspect: the twelve and the one.

There is, of course, the twelve in terms of the zodiac. I was given an article from a Christian Community priest in Europe. I went through the whole aspect of the twelve disciples and the signs of the zodiac, only to have the whole apple cart thrown upside down when I came across a handwritten letter by Michael O'Leary to Reverend Philbric talking about a lecture he had heard from Adam Bittleston. These are all names in the history of the Christian Community, in which the disciples and the zodiac were arranged completely differently. So I arrived at a place of real frustration, because there is something in all of our minds today; we want to have something straightened out. Is it two plus two? Do I translate the sentence this way or that way? We want solutions to things. I could not come to a solution that I was happy with in the translation of the disciples and the zodiac. And then I came across Luderen's book in which he said, "I'm aware of the controversy here and I'm not sure it's helpful to try to pin it down." That gave me permission to let it go.

There is also the whole piece of the biography of each disciple. I am not going to go into the biography piece, but there is a lot that can be found. I have researched numerous books, not just anthroposophic, on what people say about the disciples in terms of their background. For some, much is known, and for others not so much. I even have someone's research on how they all found their ends—who, when, and how. That is also a very interesting story. But, when you do research you cannot go down every street. It does not work. So I am going to take you down the streets that I have been able to traverse, and one of them has to do with ages. It is very interesting to look at these groupings. You find again and again an old person, a young person, and a middle-aged person. On the left of Christ, you see a very balanced representation of the three ages of humankind—old, middle, young, old, middle, and young. And you say, *Oh wonderful; it's all working out.* It's a matter of threes—perfect.

But then you look to the right, and you have again two old, two middle and two young, but they are not equal in the two groups. Here you have middle and two young, and here you have two old and a middle. This is the beginning of discovering Leonardo's genius here. He does not want it all symmetrical and in a box, and perfect. He creates this tension where you have the three ages of human beings—youth, middle age and old age—represented four times in these groups, but it is not perfectly left and right symmetrical; he mixes it up.

He does the same thing with the temperaments. You can find all the temperaments here, but it is not laid out just perfectly. If you look at the placement of the objects on the table, they are clearly not setup to be camera-ready. Things are displaced in a funny sort of way; they are not perfectly arranged on the table. Then look at the space question. There is an intensification of the three individuals here, with very little wall space behind them. The wall is pretty much blocked, and there is a very intense occupation of the space. Then we see a wide gap between John and the Christ. Again, there is this discrepancy of the background really opened up on one side, and on the other side, that is not the case. Yet you are surrounded by a kind of symmetry, and one can go into the Golden Mean and see exactly the proportions and so on.

I want to bring out this creative tension that Leonardo employs; it is intentional. I feel he wants us to wrestle with this painting, and does not want us to sit back and say, *ah, it's all been taken care of for us.* It has not been. There are many unanswered questions.

There are other aspects that I would like to bring out. There has been much study—as camera obscura was coming in, light and dark, working with shadow, and so on. As I stand here, there is a source of light on my face, and that is something that needs to be respected by the artist. When something is in the shadows, there is a reason for the shadows. Humanity, at the time of Leonardo was just about to emerge into the natural-scientific way of seeing things. Leonardo, was so aware of it; he did drawings and sketches ahead of time; he studied people and drew them.

Forgiveness and the Last Supper

For example, there is a study of Judas' hand, clutching. Although Leonardo was aware that modern natural science was dawning, when you get to the light and dark there is no external source for the light on the figure of Jesus, and there is no external reason for the darkness around Judas. Something goes on inside of us when we cannot quite figure this out.

I went back and looked at the earlier drawings and paintings of the Last Supper, and of course, they all look a bit stilted compared to Leonardo's version. But they have a place, and there was a reason for how and why they were done. Some are beautiful in my view. Almost always, though, Judas is at the end of the table, which is very interesting. We also see that he is to the right of Christ. All the disciples are at the table, arranged so that some are closer or farther back, giving a sense of depth, though they are all behind the table. Judas is there with Christ on the same side of the table, which raises a host of questions. To place your opponent there, at your right side, even though you know.

Rudolf Steiner says that there is an echo of the planetary stages—Saturn, Sun, and Moon. During the Moon stage of evolution, the gods allowed opposing forces to come into being to further human evolution—that is, knowing it would ultimately be for the good of humanity. To have your opponent or betrayer right next to you is an amazing way to work.

I am reminded of Abraham Lincoln. He had a concept that is echoed in the book *Team of Rivals* by Doris Kearns Goodwin. After he was elected, Lincoln invited his political opponents to sit in his cabinet. The philosophy behind this strategy was that it is better to engage and debate in meetings than to be surrounded by a bunch of "yes" people, which doesn't solve real problems. Those who admire and respect Lincoln, as I do, recognize in him a quality that made him more than just another president.

The notion of having your opponent at the table, the opposition right there, is something to work with. I have been called into organizations quite often to negotiate conflict mediations. I did a training course some years ago in divorce mediation. I have never counseled anybody in divorce, but I had done mediation training so I could learn to help schools better. Usually what happens is that I meet with the one individual and then with the other. One of the things I found in conflict and mediation work is that the first sign of victory, the first moment of success, is bringing the parties together to speak with each other.

I was called into a school to work with two kindergarten teachers. They were both pillars of the community in their own right. One had been trained with Margaret Meyerkort and the other by someone else. The sad thing was that they did not get along. In fact, their conflict became so great that the playground was divided between their two groups. They had separate Michaelmas festivals, separate Martinmas festivals, and separate Advent gardens, because they simply couldn't get on together. They had even built up a constituency throughout the school; there were kids who had graduated from one kindergarten, and whose parents were with that kindergarten. It was like a cold war, like a Berlin Wall, right there in the middle of the Waldorf school. It had gone on for years. One day, a new faculty chair was elected, and she somewhat naively asked, "Does it need to be this way? Can we do better?" And everyone said, "Oh, that's just the way it is. No, we can't." And she said, "No, I think we can work on this."

She called me and I sat with one teacher on her side of the Waldorf world and then with the other on her side of the Waldorf world. I heard the whole story; it went on and on and on. Then I had to meet with some people I felt represented the middle way.

You always look for the path of the heart when you are dealing with this. Sometimes, you are not the person who can bring it, but someone else can.

I remember so clearly the moment when the two women were supposed to come into the room at the same time. I sat there at the table, trembling, I did not know what would happen; either one of them could bail on me. They came in and sat down, and for a while they would not look at each other. It was all rehearsed. I had scripted the whole thing and they were playing the part, the way you recite lines when you have learned a play. Then one of them looked up and made eye contact with the other, and in that moment something thawed, and they started to speak. All I had to do was step back and monitor the situation.

I do not want to equate a Waldorf kindergarten situation with the Last Supper, but there is something really modern about the drama of the Last Supper. Having one's opponent near and being able to look at the "enemy" and being able to speak is a way of reclaiming our humanity. It is a way of restoring humanity to wholeness.

I am not a eurythmist, so you are getting a layperson's interpretation of some of these gestures. I have come across something that I found very interesting, and I would like to share it with you. Let us take these groupings and say something about the gesture of each one. I will start with Thomas, immediately to Jesus' left. His is the gesture of knowledge, insight, or cognition. It is interesting because it is knowledge, but we know that there are doubts in it. There is something in this path of knowledge that is always wrestling: *Do I know? Do I not know?* The hand gesture of Thomas is right over the left hand of Christ, which is open, is very different. Next to Thomas is James the Greater. We see in him the gesture of open-mouth surprise and vulnerability. Next is Philip. This gesture is not indicating *me*, but *self*. In Eurythmy, we often perform the "I–thou" exercise. We move around the room being the "you" gestures. It can be very exhausting, always giving, giving, giving. Then we move around with the gesture of never quite connecting with people, a very different gesture.

What I find in this group of three as a whole is the gesture of knowledge, surprise, and perhaps vulnerability and the sense of self. Because Thomas' hand is right over the hand of Christ, which is open, I understand that as the gesture of giving life. This group displays an aspect of self-knowledge that gives life.

The group at the right end is Matthew, Thaddeus, and Simon. This is about as extreme a gesture as you can imagine, even here. There is openness and a sort of quizzical quality in the gesture. After living with this group of three for a while, I saw a quality of open selflessness and awareness of the other.

At the far left is Bartholomew, James the Less, and Andrew. Andrew's gesture is a quiet *Wow*. Bartholomew displays a kind of indignation; his hands are on the table, as if to ask: What's this about? What's going on here? In living with this group of three, in the qualities of the three taken together I saw an awareness of the power of active spirit presence. Something that would cause one to say: My goodness! A kind of sensing awareness of active spirit presence—I am not trying to define but merely to characterize them.

Now we are down to this last group, seated at the right hand of Jesus. In many ways, it is the most problematic. Leonardo practiced again and again how he could portray a bent elbow going that way. It is fascinating just to observe the anatomy of all the gestures. Beginning with John, it's hard to imagine a more inward gesture: eyes closed, head down to the side, leaning over. He is almost in a place of total inner peace and quiet. He is not bothered outwardly by this. He has gone deep down within himself; the pools run very deep there. Next is Peter, out of order since he is leaning over behind Judas. Peter is whispering in John's ear, saying something in confidence that the whole group cannot hear, but it is a whisper, which reinforces this inner quality. When you whisper, you are more withdrawn. The third figure in the group, Judas, is recoiling and reaching for the bread. His right hand is clenched. It is also inward, but in a more physically inward sense. It is not coming from inner peace but from a physical recoiling. This group as a whole shows creative tension of inner and outer and focus on the inner realities. I would describe the overall gesture of this group as inwardness of soul. John rules the day here.

You may wonder where I am going with all this. The interesting thing is that, long before I got into the Last Supper in this way, I had done much study of servant leadership. Robert Greenleaf was perhaps the greatest writer on this. I have read his books, which present a whole field of study on the topic. He took his cue from Herman Hesse and the book *Journey to the East*, a description of a person walking at the end of the caravan in the dust. He has a staff and wears ragged clothes. You can imagine the cattle, the dung, and the people who are lame or cannot quite keep up. The very end of a caravan.... The raggle taggle remains of a long procession of wagons, people, dignitaries.

This man is at the very end, and he looks perhaps like the poorest, humblest, and simplest of them all. Whenever something happens, one of the animals is lame or somebody is thirsty, that individual lends a hand. Other than that, he is just an unremarkable hanger-on at the end of the caravan.

Hesse then, in his way, goes to another chapter. You are in a scene of a sort of high priestly order, a palace, a great building, and there is the wise elder teacher presiding. It turns out that the servant leader at the back of the caravan and the high priest are one and the same person.

Greenleaf took this image of the humblest, the servant, and the highest, the priest leader. He took this into his study of servant leadership. He wrote pages and pages, and much has been written about servant leadership. My *Aha* moment came when I recalled the key tenets of servant leadership and realized that Leonardo had them all in *The Last Supper!* A servant leader is someone who has a high level of self-awareness and has practiced self-knowledge. A servant leader is someone who is very aware of the other, is not there out of personal ambition but to really help those in need, and is someone who works with the periphery. A servant leader is someone who has an inwardness of soul, and someone who has an active spirit mission. We call it now mission driven, value driven; we have all kinds of language around this in mainstream leadership development texts.

My *Aha* moment was all of this literature in servant leadership that I found was echoed in Leonardo's *Last Supper*. The qualities of not any one disciple, not any one grouping, but going back to that opening quote of this chapter, the idea that the" whole" represents the complete picture of humanity. For me at least, this was really meaningful. In our work today—Camphill communities, Waldorf schools, biodynamic farms, and new therapies—we are trying not only to bring new content, but also trying to model new ways of working together. Servant leadership is a way for us to show the world that it is not just our ideas, but it is also our practices that can make a difference. That was a step for me in my work with *The Last Supper*.

Then finally, after all of that, I decided to give myself a treat. I went back to reading some biographies of Leonardo da Vinci and read the lecture Rudolf Steiner gave in Berlin on February

23, 1913. It is a treat when you can find an entire lecture by Rudolf Steiner on your subject; usually there are only references here and there. I went over this lecture again and what I came up with was a third echo of the themes that I have brought forward in this book, now played out in the life of Leonardo. If you study his biography, you see much of the drama of the Last Supper; you see much of these qualities at work yet again. And when you come to something again and again, you start to approach what I call *truthfulness*. There is something there that you can start to say, "Yes, this rings with integrity."

Here are just a few highlights from Leonardo's life. These are well known; I am not going to go into his childhood. What I want to bring out is this self-portrait from the end of his life. Rudolf Steiner actually starts early on talking about this face and what it communicates: a kind of wisdom but also disappointment, a kind of hardened discipline, frustration, and yet one can still see the footprints of greatness in this self-portrait.

Throughout his biography, one sees how he worked with observations of people, how he would follow somebody for hours, trying to get the gesture. In so doing he had to practice a kind of *unconditional hospitality of the soul*. In these sketches, Leonardo took the same person and experimented by making the jaw bigger or smaller. He tried drawing the same hands again and again in different ways. This was a pursuit of observable, sense perceptible information that could then be transposed into his drawings. He was a scientist trying very hard to understand and he used his *senses* to their full capacity.

One sees in Leonardo's life how he was drawn into one project after another, partly because his commissions varied so much. He was paid by one person and then they would stop paying and he had to go to somebody else; he had to move around. He was inventing war machines and flying objects, he was doing paintings, a great workhorse. Often these projects were never completed, which is another quality to bear in mind. Then you have Leonardo's style of working with *The Last Supper*. Here is what Steiner had to say about it:

> He often went and sat on the scaffolding and brooded for hours in front of the wall. He would then take a brush, make a few strokes, and go away again. Sometimes he went and only stared at the picture before leaving again. When he was painting the Christ figure, his hand trembled. (Steiner, lecture on Leonardo, p. 21)

For me, that is again a clue into the soul life. Leonardo realized that he was doing something so great, he stood there and, sometimes totally immobilized, could not move. Other times, his hand was trembling. He had great difficulty completing Judas and the face of Christ. There is a humorous story about the prior who said to Leonardo numerous times, "Can you just finish it? Get this thing done!" And Leonardo said, "I just can't find a way to render Judas." The prior responded, "Well just do it. Get it done!" And Leonardo said, "If you keep pushing me, I will use you as my model" (King, p. 127).

Then Leonardo got a little space to work for a while, but there was still a feeling of dissatisfaction. As he was working on *The Last Supper,* he felt that he was unable to do justice to the theme. As time passed, Leonardo felt increasingly powerless. He felt a sense of being unable to do what he had promised. Of course, he did finish it, but his sense of frustration and the difficulty in the whole thing then lived itself out in the history of the work of art itself. We know that it started to deteriorate within a few years; we know that it was suffered from the effects of bombs during World War II—at one point, it was used for target practice. Then the monks in the priory decided they wanted a door underneath, so they just dug away a part of it and made a door, the top of which can be seen in the image of *The Last Supper* on page 120. The destiny of the painting mirrors a little bit the destiny of the artist creating it: this frustration and this troubled quality.

Finally, Rudolf Steiner gets to the essence of what he is trying to say about Leonardo which is that he really stood at a threshold moment. Humanity was about to enter the time of the consciousness soul; it was about to be at a time when natural science would really reign supreme. It was also *a time in which humanity would need to come to grips with evil and all its manifestations.* (Steiner, many references in From Symptom to Reality). Leonardo was already one step into that realm with his drawings and his scientific work. In the time of natural science, humanity would develop a great longing for the spiritual heritage and realize that we cannot understand everything just by measuring the weight and the height and the shape and the color of things. That there must be more to life than what we see with the senses. But all of that was living in Leonardo and was yet to fully develop in subsequent centuries.

What Leonardo drew on was his past life experiences and his awareness that something was working intuitively within him—an understanding that came from the ancient times, from Greece and beyond. (Steiner, Leonardo lecture, p. 20) It was living within him but he was not able to bring it to full consciousness and come to peace within himself. It was a stirring within him, the way we often have an intuition. "I probably should go home early today. I think something's going on. I need to check in with someone. I need to make a phone call." We have this kind of surging within of an intuition.

For Leonardo, it was this welling up from his past lives, this richness that lived in his soul, and yet he could not quite find a way to always make it happen. Even with the tools he had at his disposal and the dawning of new consciousness among humankind, he still was not quite there. He stood on a precipice. We see in his self-portrait someone who has really weathered, more than just sixty two years. It is more than just sixty two years of normal life. There was something that had been going on in the soul of this person that was far greater than the passage of time.

Rudolf Steiner begins and ends his lecture with this notion of bitterness and frustration in the face of genius. This is an interesting way to draw everything together, because what happens then is we have the themes that we have covered of betrayal. Leonardo was betrayed again and again: people did not pay him, disappointment, lost friendships. We have the theme of forgiveness. When you look not just at *The Last Supper* but in many of his paintings, there is a kind of absolving and rounding out and making beautiful again what had been so difficult. Then we see the threshold experiences. *The Last Supper,* for me, has become a threshold experience. Those questions: who is it here at this table? Who will betray? This is the moment of the threshold of consciousness of betrayal and what is about to come right after the Last Supper. That moment. The threshold moment that has changed the whole history of the world. That possibility through the crucifixion and so on that has been given to humanity. There is a threshold moment in the Last Supper.

Our lives today are filled with threshold experiences. I am convinced that modern human beings live through numerous threshold experiences—some of them minor, some of them larger. Betrayal and forgiveness are some of them, but there are many other instances of threshold moments, such as near-death experiences. For the victim and sometimes even for the perpetrator, an act of violence can be a painful threshold experience that leaves a mark that years cannot erase. Trauma continues to echo with inner and outer manifestations. Those who have suffered trauma continue to live on the threshold for the rest of their lives. Nevertheless, there can be a certain amount of healing as a result of counseling, artistic therapy, and other means.

One could say, certainly in regard to genocide and war atrocities, that large groups of humanity have suffered betrayal of the highest order. The suffering calls to humanity for new consciousness, new awareness of our fragility as humans and our susceptibility to acts of violence.

This question is larger than the scope of this book (or perhaps any book): how do we meet our modern threshold experiences? I would like to just suggest that the Last Supper gives us some possibilities, some pathways, to an answer. Through working with self-knowledge and developing self-awareness, developing awareness of the other, inwardness of soul, and active "spirit presencing," we have some possibilities for meeting threshold experiences in this age of the consciousness soul.

Yet, I would like to add one more essential quality if we are to sustain ourselves going forward: hope. Hope has lived with humanity for a long time, especially since the crucifixion. It is essential to servant leadership. One has to believe in other people despite it all; one has to have hope.

When our son Thomas suffered a terrible accident of a stick going into his eye at two-and-a-half year of age, we rushed him to Albany Medical Center. A team of doctors examined him and said that it was hopeless. They were going to have to remove the eye, saying that he might even lose the other eye and be blind. We were distraught. There was one man who stood out as advanced in both years and his career—indeed, Dr. Stasior was close to retirement. He stood before us as a sort of Leonardo among his team of physicians. After everyone had spoken, we were sitting there as parents, tears streaming down our faces, thinking of our son losing his sight and wondering why this had to happen: Why us? Then he said, "There's a chance that if we operate and seal the eye for three months, and if we bathe it in antibiotics, there's a chance we can rescue his sight." Then he paused and said, "If there's hope, one always has to go with hope." And we agreed to go ahead.

Dr. Stasior performed the operation, which took six hours. Three months went by, and we had no idea how or if it was progressing because of the bandage. The amazing thing—the karma of this story—was that Thomas' grandmother had specialized in curative eurythmy for eyes. He had been placed in a family in which one member, his beloved grandmother, had chosen to specialize in color and movement therapy. She had designed a studio in her house that was set up especially to work with the colors. After the eye patch was removed, we started using plant-based medicine drops from the Weleda pharmacy, and Thomas' grandmother started doing the curative eurythmy for the eye.

We returned to see Dr. Stasior and sat in the waiting room. You can imagine we were on the edges of our chairs waiting to hear the news. When he came out to the waiting room, he was not doing a song and dance and kicking his legs. The utmost example of humility, he just walked out quietly and in a quiet voice said, "We still have a physical basis for sight. Now the question is, can we regain some use of the eye." That was all he said. So modest, but his hope and skill as a doctor had saved the day. Thomas is now a happy father and a successful investment advisor.

In the end, this book on nonviolent education is about the notion of *hope*. As long as we have children on this Earth, there will be hope. We need only follow their lead, allow their interests to lead us back to nature, and let their joy in learning inspire us to parent and teach as suggested throughout this book. May we surround them with unconditional hospitality and warmth. May we protect childhood and the rites of passage as unique features of renewal. And may we give children the gift of the arts, all of which give us tools toward resiliency and healthy development of character.

Much to my joy, it turns out Rudolf Steiner also ended his previously mentioned lecture on Leonardo with a message of hope.

> ...from the sunset the promise and the hope of the dawn arises for us. The relation of our souls to human evolution must always be such that we say to ourselves: All progress takes this course; wherever what has been created falls into ruin, we know that from that ruin new life will always blossom forth." (Steiner, Leonardo p. 27)

14

Advocates of Nonviolence

"Let people overcome anger by love; let them overcome evil by good; let them overcome the greedy by liberality and the liar by truth! For hatred will never cease through hatred; it ceases through love; this is an ancient rule. Speak the truth; do not yield to anger; give, if you are asked. Through these three steps you will become divine."
—The Buddha

With these words we see how the condition of our society is so intimately bound up with the human condition. Anger, hatred, and violence must yield if we are to have a more peaceful world. An air force, army, or navy can never be large enough to supplant the basic need for right human conduct. It is humans who start conflict, use weapons, and pay a most precious price in war. If we want a less violent society, we have to start with the human condition.

Food, shelter, medical care, and a good education are essential basics for good conduct, as desperation can lead many a good person to commit desperate acts. We need a complete redirection in our priorities: sharing wealth with those less fortunate, at home and around the world.

As basic as food and shelter is the need for an education that allows the possibility for work and the dignity that comes with gainful employment. But it is not enough to just put every child behind a desk. The quality of instruction and the collective experience in what we call "school" makes all the difference.

Too much abstract information, rote learning, and boredom can inoculate a child toward further education. Awakening curiosity and imagination, real problem solving, meaningful projects, and critical thinking can become lifelong resources that are transferable to many work situations even years later. Far too much emphasis has been placed on the transfer of information and retention assessment. Too little attention is given to the art of teaching and how children are more successful when taught in age-appropriate ways.

Waldorf education features three keywords that can give context to much of what happens in a healthy learning environment: truth, beauty, and goodness. The young child needs to experience the basic goodness of the teacher and a stable environment. The child in the early grades needs to experience the beauty of the natural world and learn to create beauty with his/her own hands. And the adolescent needs to develop passion for the truth. Each of these three qualities can become instruments for peace.

Few have demonstrated the force of truth better than Gandhi:

> Satyagraha was the Sanskritic combination Gandhi later chose as a name for his way of life and of action—"Truth" and "Force," in literal translation. Yet for quite some time Gandhi continued to use what was easily the most unsuitable rendition of his in English, namely, "passive resistance." This dilemma has never been resolved: "Truth force" as a term has nowhere come close to having the power of a slogan in the West. "Militant nonviolence" (the term, I think, preferred by Martin Luther King) is at least descriptive of the attitude and the action of the Satyagrahi, but it fails to suggest the spiritual origin or nonviolent courage in Gandhi's "truth." I will speak of the "leverage of truth" when, in addition to truth and force, I want to suggest the skillful use of a sensitive instrument. For it must be obvious that it is the challenge of our generation to understand, as far as psychological assumptions permit, what Gandhi calls truth as an actual force in mental life, the kind of force that

> "moves mountains." A lever, I admit, is a hopelessly primitive analogy in an electronic age. But whatever we will do with it in the future setting, Satyagraha did have its origins in a technological imagery in which the body was still part of the tool; and it will be seen that even today the more direct uses of Satyagraha always include the body and the meeting of bodies: the facing of the opponent " eye to eye," the linking of arms in defensive and advancing phalanxes, the body "on the line": all these confrontations symbolize the conviction that the solidarity of unarmed bodies remains a leverage and a measure, even against the cold and mechanized gadgetry of the modern state.
>
> At the beginning of an age, then, when man is apt to sacrifice the threefold instrumentality of his body, his mind, and his soul to the clever complexity of his own inventions, Gandhi, as we shall see, strove for the naked clarity of all three. (Erikson, p. 198)

This notion of the threefold instrumentality of the body is fascinating. Rather than becoming totally enmeshed in the complexity of our own inventions, Gandhi calls for a kind of "clearing" in which the essential purposes are once again made transparent. We want human beings to be good and to treat each other with respect. We need to use the leverage of truth to achieve a more just society.

Howard Zinn, in his book *The Power of Nonviolence: Writings by Advocates of Peace* has collected a wide variety of advocates who speak to the need for an entirely new way of thinking:

> Did we commit terrorist acts to "send a message" to terrorists? We have responded that way before. It is the old way of thinking, the old way of acting, and it has never worked. Reagan bombed Libya, Bush made war on Iraq, and Clinton bombed Afghanistan, and also a pharmaceutical plant in the Sudan, to "send a message" to terrorists. And then comes this horror in New York and Washington. Isn't it clear by now that sending a message to terrorists through violence doesn't work; it only leads to more terrorism?... We need

new ways of thinking. A $300 billion military budget has not given us security. American military bases all over the world, our warships on every ocean, have not given us security.... Our security can only come by using our national wealth, not for guns, planes, bombs, but for the health and welfare of our people—for free medical care for everyone, education and housing, guaranteed decent wages, and a clean environment for all. We cannot be secure by limiting our liberties, as some of our political leaders are demanding, but only by expanding them. (Zinn, viii–ix)

Ralph Waldo Emerson makes this interesting observation:

> Every nation and every man instantly surround themselves with a material apparatus which exactly corresponds to their moral state, or their state of thought.... We surround ourselves always, according to our freedom and ability, with true images of ourselves in things, whether it be ships or books or cannon or churches. The standing army, the arsenal, the camp and the gibbet do not appertain to man. They only serve as an index to show where man is now. (Emerson, pp. 544–545)

And this, he maintains, is related to the stages in the development of human consciousness:

> War and peace thus resolve themselves into a mercury of the state of cultivation. At a certain stage of his progress, the man fights, if he be of a sound body and mind. At a certain higher stage he makes no offensive demonstration, but is alert to repel injury, and of an unconquerable heart. At a still higher stage he comes into the region of holiness; passion has passed away from him; his warlike nature is all converted into an active medicinal principle; he sacrifices himself and accepts with alacrity wearisome tasks of denial and charity; but being attacked, he bears it and turns the other cheek, as one engaged, throughout his being, no longer to the service of an individual but to the common soul of all men.... Nor, in the next place, is the peace principle to be carried into effect by fear. It can never be defended,

it can never be executed, by cowards. Everything great must be done in the spirit of greatness. The manhood that has been in war must be transferred to the cause of peace, before war can lose its charm, and peace be vulnerable to men. (ibid., pp. 548-549)

...and peace be vulnerable to men—a curious use of the term *vulnerable*, which one can also understand as *valuable* or *precious*. And to overcome hindrances we need to confront the soul conditions of fear, a root cause of aggressive behavior. Scott Nearing expresses this so well:

> I regard war as a social disease, a social curse, and I believe that we should stamp war out. To my mind the greater curse of war is not that people are killed and injured, not that property is destroyed. That happens every day in peace times as well as in war times. To my mind that great curse of war is that it is built on fear and hate.
> Now, fear and hate are primitive passions; the savages in the woods are intimidated by fear and hate. They do not belong in civilized society. In civilized society, for fear and hate we substitute constructive purposes and love. It is their positive virtues. When we fear things, we draw back from them. When we hate things, we want to destroy them.
> In civilized society, instead of drawing away from things, and wanting to destroy them, we want to pull things together and build them up. Fear and hate are negatives. Peace and love are positives, and form the forces upon which civilizations is built....
> I stand before you today as an advocate of economic justice and world brotherhood, and peace among all men. (Zinn, pp. 42-44)

Building things up instead of destroying them is what education is all about. But it takes strenuous inner work and personal discipline:

> The perfect state is reached only when mind and body and speech are in proper coordination. But it is always a case

of intense mental struggle. It is not that I am incapable of anger, for instance, but I succeed on almost all occasions to keep my feelings under control. Whatever may be the result, there is always in me a conscious struggle for following the law of nonviolence, deliberately and ceaselessly. Such a struggle leaves one stronger for it. Nonviolence is a weapon of the strong. With the weak it might easily be hypocrisy. Fear and love are contradictory terms. Love is reckless in giving away, oblivious as to what it gets in return. Love wrestles with the world as with the self and ultimately gains a mastery over all other feelings. May daily experience, as of those who are working with me, is that every problem lends itself to solution if we are determined to make the law of truth and nonviolence the law of life. For truth and nonviolence are, to me, faces of the same coin. (Zinn, p. 46)

Just as Emerson influenced Gandhi, both men provided a foundation for the work of Martin Luther King, as seen in these words of the great civil rights leader:

Here is the true meaning and value of compassion and nonviolence, when it helps us to see the enemy's point of view, to hear his questions, to know of his assessment of ourselves. For from his view we may indeed see the basic weaknesses of our own condition, and if we are mature, we may learn and grow and profit from the wisdom of the brothers who are called the opposition....

I am convinced that, if we are to get on the right side of the world revolution, we as a nation must undergo a radical revolution of values. When machines and computers, profit and property rights, are considered more important than people, the giant triplets of racism, materialism, and militarism are incapable of being conquered....

America, the richest and most powerful nation in the world, can well lead the way in this revolution of values. There is nothing, except a tragic death wish, to prevent us from reordering our priorities, so that the pursuit of peace will take precedence over the pursuit of war. There is nothing to keep us from molding a recalcitrant status quo until we have fashioned it into a brotherhood....

If we do not act we shall surely be dragged down the long, dark and shameful corridors of time reserved for those who possess power without compassion, might without morality, and strength without sight.

Now let us begin. Now let us re-dedicate ourselves to the long and bitter, but beautiful, struggle for a new world. This is the calling of the sons of God, and our brothers wait eagerly for our response. Shall we say the odds are too great? Shall we tell them the struggle is too hard? Will our message be that the forces of American life militate against their arrival as full men, and we send our deepest regrets? Or will there be another message, of longing, of hope, of solidarity with their yearnings, of commitment to their cause, whatever the cost? The choice is ours, and though we might prefer it otherwise we must choose in this crucial moment of human history. (Zinn, pp, 118–124)

These words ring forth even after so many years, and seem more relevant today than ever before! Of the many gems in the above lines, I want to comment particularly on the phrase "radical revolution of values," for this is where the third aspect of Waldorf for nonviolence comes into play. Buddha helped focus our attention on the need for improving the human condition (goodness), and Emerson and Gandhi spoke eloquently on the power of truth.

Most people tend to associate the development of values with family, church, or community traditions. All these are of course important. I would like to develop this theme from a more unconventional approach, namely the role of aesthetics, or beauty, in support of value formation. This is a highly individualized process that takes place within each child, often unseen, and certainly unrecognized by those who design our standardized tests. Yet it goes to the heart of an education dedicated to nonviolence.

In the above citation from Martin Luther King, we have the words, "those who possess power without compassion, might without morality, and strength without sight." These are people without guiding moral principles, politicians, and others who use and abuse rather than serve. Let us start with the last words regarding "strength without sight." To be able to see requires perception that is unclouded by personal prejudice and assumptions. One has to clear the line of vision to be able to see what the phenomena or the person is actually presenting. Rather than judge someone by ethnicity or race, direct perception requires that one be inwardly silent so as to let the perception of the person really speak. There is no better training for this than the visual arts, in which one tries, for example, to draw a tree, as it truly is, not as one thinks it should be. If one is able to accurately draw a hemlock, aspen, or birch, the essence of that tree can shine forth. The important result is not so much a piece of paper with a drawing that may be more or less successful. Rather, the valuable outcome is *the capacity to see*. One has to let go of self and preconceptions to really see the other. Thus Waldorf schools emphasize phenomenology as the doorway into science education; perception before conceptualization. This is the opposite of "strength without sight" in which one postulates, assumes, or one group or individual tries to impose values and standards upon another.

Then there is the phrase "might without morality." We all know from world affairs today what this is all about, yet are we doing enough to enhance the cause of morality? In so many instances we have ceded the cause of morality to organized religion, and in the attempt to uphold the separation of church and state we have given up on any notion that schools might still play a role in the development of morality. I understand the reasons for separating what is usually called moral education from schools, as much harm can be done under this banner, yet I would like to redefine education for morality and show that there is still a place for character development.

When a child does drama in school with costumes, props, and lights, there is a chance to become someone else, to try on a new character. Our six children have been in a variety of plays in their Waldorf schools, and they have always enjoyed the excitement and challenge of learning a new part. A good role can help one try on something entirely new, especially if the director does some "pedagogical casting," namely suggesting a part that can provide an opportunity for personal growth. Adopting a new character actually helps one's own character development.

Much drama contends with the age old issues of role confusion, tragedy, and comedy that looks at ordinary things in a new light. In short, a good play is not just about entertainment. The beauty of the final production masks a lot of human development (and sometimes the anguish of the director along the way!). But in dealing with interpersonal relationships on stage, with death and remorse, with success and failure, drama provides an opportunity to *earn a place on the stage, to achieve through hard work, to find a voice,* not through might, position, wealth, or rank, but through passionate struggle. Drama develops character and a foundation for wise choices later in life. This is the foundation of moral action.

Then finally we have the Martin Luther King phrase "power without compassion." Here again, aesthetics can help. When painting, it is not just a matter to throwing some color on the page. A painting class as taught in a Waldorf school allows the color to speak to the soul of the child. Red meeting yellow is so different than when it meets blue; feelings come into play. When I painted with my class, one could often hear a pin drop on the floor. They were so intent on living into the colors that their faces radiated devotion. When children paint again and again, they develop emotional intelligence, sensitivity to new experiences, and compassion.

Power without compassion is the raw exercise of will without heart. Painting, singing, and all the arts foster compassion that can guide and instruct toward right action. As Vladimir Solovyov said, "beauty will save the world." Truth, beauty, and goodness are the hallmarks of an education that strives toward nonviolent solutions to our modern challenges at home and globally. Then humanity will have another chance at fulfilling the ideals so needed today:

> Let people overcome anger by love; let them overcome evil by good; let them overcome the greedy by liberality and the liar by truth! For hatred will never cease through hatred; it ceases through love; this is an ancient rule. Speak the truth; do not yield to anger; give, if you are asked; through these three steps you will become divine.

15

A Bill of Rights for Children

We hold these rights to belong to all children, regardless of ethnic, religious, or economic background. All children on Earth are our Children, our collective responsibility and sacred trust. They are often unable to speak for themselves, to vote, or to make decisions vital to their interests; the adult community needs to protect and cherish every child. Collectively, we need to guarantee certain inalienable rights for all children:

1. The experience of childhood, as represented in free play, recess, safety, and companionship with others;
2. Access to the great outdoors, the wonders of Nature, and all the benefits of sensory education;
3. Good nutrition;
4. A developmentally appropriate education;
5. Exposure to and practice in arts such as movement, color, music, drama, and so on as vital to developing emotional intelligence;
6. Experiential learning through projects and creative activities that support the balanced development of thinking, feeling, and doing;
7. The joy of storytelling that develops awareness of multicultural people and cultures around the world and throughout history;
8. Teachers who are inspired to teach;
9. All children need and deserve rites of passage that celebrate transitions and recognition as emerging individuals.

Works Cited

Albrecht, Karl. *Social Intelligence: The New Science of Success*. Hoboken, NJ; Wiley/Pfeiffer, 2007.

Bottcher, Cordelia. "The Circle of the Twelve Apostles," in *Die Christengemeinschaft*, 1991–2.

Burkhour, Cindy, and Joan Almon. "Play and Playgrounds," in Human Kinetics (ed.). *Inclusive Recreation: Programs and Services for Diverse Populations*. Champaign, IL: Human Kinetics, 2010.

Emerson, Ralph Waldo. *Essays, First and Second Series* (address on war). New York: Hearst, 1914

Erikson, Erik H. *Gandhi's Truth: On the Origins of Militant Nonviolence*. New York: Norton, 1969.

Gladwell, Malcolm. *Outliers: The Story of Success*. New York: Little, Brown, 2008.

Goodwin, Doris Kearns. *Team of Rivals: The Political Genius of Abraham Lincoln*. New York: Simon and Schuster, 2005.

Hugo, Victor. *Les Misérables* (tr. L. Fahnestock and N. MacAfee). New York: Signet Classics, 2013.

King, Ross. *Leonardo and the Last Supper*. New York: Bloomsbury, 2012.

Kühlewind, Georg. "Forgiving," in *Journal for Anthroposophy*. Ann Arbor, MI, 2013.

Ladwein, Michael. *Leonardo da Vinci: The Last Supper*. Forest Row, UK: Temple Lodge, 2006.

Lashlie, Celia. *He'll Be Okay: Growing Gorgeous Boys into Good Men*. Auckland: HarperCollins, 2005.

Louv, Richard. *Last Child in the Woods: Saving Our Children from Nature-deficit Disorder*. Chapel Hill, NC: Algonquin, 2008.

Lusseyran, Jacques. *Against the Pollution of the I*. New York: Myrin Institute, 1975.

Montagu, Ashley. *Growing Young* (2nd ed.). Westport, CT: Greenwood, 1989.

Pohl, Christine D. *Making Room: Recovering Hospitality as a Christian Tradition*. Grand Rapids, MI: Eerdmans, 1999.

Prokofieff, Sergei O. *The Occult Significance of Forgiveness*, Forest Row, UK, Temple Lodge, 1991.

Richards, M. C. *Towards Wholeness: Rudolf Steiner Education in America*. Middletown, CT: Wesleyan, 1980.

Soesman, Albert. *Our Twelve Senses: How Healthy Senses Refresh the Soul*. Stroud, UK: Hawthorn, 2006.

Steiner, Rudolf. *Anthroposophical Leading Thoughts: Anthroposophy as a Path of Knowledge: The Michael Mystery*. Forest Row, UK: Rudolf Steiner Press, 1973.

———. *Approaching the Mystery of Golgotha* ("The Four Sacrifices of Christ"). Great Barrington, MA: SteinerBooks, 2006.

———. *Education for Adolescents*. Hudson, NY: Anthroposophic Press, 1996.

———. *Evil: Selected Lectures*. Forest Row, UK: Rudolf Steiner Press, 1997.

———. *The Fifth Gospel: From the Akashic Record*. Forest Row, UK: Rudolf Steiner Press, 1968.

———. *From Symptom to Reality: In Modern History*. Forest Row, UK: Rudolf Steiner Press, 2015.

———. "Leonardo da Vinci: His Spiritual Greatness at the Turning Point of the New Age" (lecture in Berlin, Feb. 13, 1913).

———. *The Lord's Prayer: An Esoteric Study*. London: Theosophical Publishing, 2010; cf. Rudolf Steiner. *The Lord's Prayer: An Esoteric Study*. Forest Row, UK: Rudolf Steiner Press, 2008.

———. *Metamorphoses of the Soul: Paths of Experience*, vol. 2. London: Rudolf Steiner Press, 1983 (current edition: *Transforming the Soul*, vol 2. Forest Row, UK: Rudolf Steiner Press, 2005).

———. "The Structure of the Lord's Prayer." London: Rudolf Steiner Press, 1971.

———. *The Temple Legend: Freemasonry and Related Occult Movements: From the Contents of the Esoteric School*. Forest Row, UK: Rudolf Steiner Press, 2000 (lect. 2).

Zinn, Howard (ed.). *The Power of Nonviolence: Writings by Advocates of Peace*. Boston, MA: Beacon Press, 2002.

Acknowledgements

I am grateful to colleagues in Waldorf education who have graciously given me their time and wisdom for background interviews: Signe Motter, Karl Shurman, and Susan Weber. Likewise, I want to recognize and thank my Antioch research assistants, Sarah (Tiffany) Kopp for her early editing help, and Ann Pasquinelly for typing the longer quotations. I am, as always, grateful to Jens Jensen for his editing and to SteinerBooks for their perseverance in a challenging publishing world, their dedication to their authors, and for being the largest publisher of anthroposophic books in the English-speaking world.

CPSIA information can be obtained
at www.ICGtesting.com
Printed in the USA
BVOW03s1339211117
500989BV00001B/1/P